CHILDREN'S LITERATURE

Children's Literature is an accessible introduction to this engaging field. Carrie Hintz offers a defining conceptual overview of children's literature that presents its competing histories, its cultural contexts, and the theoretical debates it has instigated.

Positioned within the wider field of adult literary, film, and television culture, this book also covers:

- Ideological and political movements
- Children's literature in the age of globalization
- Postcolonial literature, ecocriticism, and animal studies

Each chapter includes a case study featuring well-known authors and titles, including *Charlotte's Web*, Edward Lear, and Laura Ingalls Wilder. With a comprehensive glossary and further reading, this book is invaluable for anyone studying Children's Literature.

Carrie Hintz is Associate Professor of English at Queens College and The Graduate Center, City University of New York, USA.

THE NEW CRITICAL IDIOM

SERIES EDITOR: JOHN DRAKAKIS, UNIVERSITY OF STIRLING

The New Critical Idiom is an invaluable series of introductory guides to today's critical terminology. Each book:

- provides a handy, explanatory guide to the use (and abuse) of the term;
- offers an original and distinctive overview by a leading literary and cultural critic;
- relates the term to the larger field of cultural representation.

With a strong emphasis on clarity, lively debate and the widest possible breadth of examples, *The New Critical Idiom* is an indispensable approach to key topics in literary studies.

The Sublime
Second edition
Philip Shaw

Satire
John T. Gilmore

Race
Martin Orkin with Alexa Alice Joubin

Trauma
Stef Craps and Lucy Bond

Children's Literature
Carrie Hintz

Pastoral
Second edition
Terry Gifford

For more information about this series, please visit: www.routledge.com/literature/series/SE0155

CHILDREN'S LITERATURE

Carrie Hintz

LONDON AND NEW YORK

First published 2020
by Routledge
2 Park Square, Milton Park, Abingdon, Oxon OX14 4RN

and by Routledge
52 Vanderbilt Avenue, New York, NY 10017

Routledge is an imprint of the Taylor & Francis Group, an informa business

© 2020 Carrie Hintz

The right of Carrie Hintz to be identified as author of this work has been asserted by her in accordance with sections 77 and 78 of the Copyright, Designs and Patents Act 1988.

All rights reserved. No part of this book may be reprinted or reproduced or utilised in any form or by any electronic, mechanical, or other means, now known or hereafter invented, including photocopying and recording, or in any information storage or retrieval system, without permission in writing from the publishers.

Trademark notice: Product or corporate names may be trademarks or registered trademarks, and are used only for identification and explanation without intent to infringe.

British Library Cataloguing-in-Publication Data
A catalogue record for this book is available from the British Library

Library of Congress Cataloging-in-Publication Data
A catalog record has been requested for this book

ISBN: 978-1-138-66794-5 (hbk)
ISBN: 978-1-138-66795-2 (pbk)
ISBN: 978-1-315-61883-8 (ebk)

Typeset in Times New Roman
by Taylor & Francis Books

Contents

Series Editor's Preface vii
Acknowledgements viii

Introduction 1

1 Definitions 7

2 Children's literature: early and global histories 41

3 Children's literature and the political 76

4 Theories and methodologies 103

5 Children's literature and the global and natural world 136

Conclusion 156

Glossary 159
Bibliography 166
Index 181

SERIES EDITOR'S PREFACE

The New Critical Idiom is a series of introductory books which seeks to extend the lexicon of literary terms in order to address the radical changes that have taken place in the study of literature during the last decades of the 20th century. The aim is to provide clear, well-illustrated accounts of the full range of terminology currently in use, and to evolve histories of its changing usage.

The current state of the discipline of literary studies is one where there is considerable debate concerning basic questions of terminology. This involves, among other things, the boundaries which distinguish the literary from the non-literary; the position of literature within the larger sphere of culture; the relationship between literatures of different cultures; and questions concerning the relation of literary to other cultural forms within the context of interdisciplinary studies.

It is clear that the field of literary criticism and theory is a dynamic and heterogeneous one. The present need is for individual volumes on terms which combine clarity of exposition with an adventurousness of perspective and a breadth of application. Each volume will contain as part of its apparatus some indication of the direction in which the definitions of particular terms are likely to move, as well as expanding the disciplinary boundaries within which some of these terms have been traditionally contained. This will involve some re-situation of terms within the larger field of cultural representation, and will introduce examples from the area of film and the modern media in addition to examples from a variety of literary texts.

Acknowledgements

Many people helped in the development of this book. I am grateful to John Drakakis for his thoughtful, rigorous, and wise editorial feedback over many years. It is an honour to be part of the NCI series. Many thanks to Ruth Hilsdon, Zoë Meyer, and Polly Dodson at Routledge for their patience through the very long process of crafting this book. Thanks as well to copyeditor Roger Browning and production editor Louise Peterken. I am grateful for their efficiency and professionalism throughout the editorial and production process.

Jason Tougaw responded to multiple drafts of the manuscript; his insights made it an infinitely stronger book. Thank you, Jason, for championing scholarship that reaches out to every reader, and for embodying that in your own books. I am also grateful for the kind encouragement of Glenn Burger, Steve Kruger, and Karen Weingarten. Eric L. Tribunella is a boundless inspiration as a colleague, interlocutor, and scholar; I learn from him constantly. Warm thanks to Balaka Basu, Katherine R. Broad, Elaine Ostry, Keridiana Chez, JoJo Karlin, Meira Levinson, Dainy Bernstein, Mikayla Zagoria-Moffet, Sara Remedios, Heather Zuber, Elissa Myers, and Sarah Winters for lively conversation about children's and YA literature. A special thanks to Christian Lewis for sharing his knowledge of disability studies with me, to Kristi Fleetwood for her insights into children's literature and popular culture, Elaine Housseas for her help in navigating many fundamental texts in the discipline, and Olivia Wood for her steady assistance.

Access to the Frederick Lewis Allen Room was indispensable for this project. Thank you to Melanie Locay and the staff at the New York Public Library for this haven of quiet productivity, and for all of the resources you made available.

Thank you to Carol and Art Hintz and to the entire Hamilton clan for much encouragement along the way! My greatest thanks go to Peter Hamilton. Without his patience, love, and support this book would never have been finished, and I can't think of a better person to celebrate with now that it is done.

INTRODUCTION

In *The Magician's Book: A Skeptic's Adventures in Narnia* (2008), journalist and critic Laura Miller describes her childhood encounter with C.S. Lewis's *The Lion, The Witch and the Wardrobe* (1950): 'First, I want a place I've read about in a book to really exist, and second, I want to be able to go there. I want this so much I'm pretty sure the misery of not getting it will kill me. For the rest of my life, I will never want anything quite so much again' (Miller 2008, 3). Miller's passion for the entire *Narnia* series is shaken later in childhood by the discovery of elements of which she was initially ignorant: an explicit Christian symbolism that, as a non-believer, she bitterly resented, experiencing it as a kind of deceit. As an adult, Miller became newly aware of the series' troubling racial politics, as seen in the demonization of the Calormenes, Narnia's enemies from the south-east, described as dark-skinned characters and read by many as a caricature of people of Middle-Eastern descent. Some of Lewis's sexist treatment of the female Pevensies also gave her pause, especially the fate of Susan, dismissed in *The Last Battle* as 'no longer a friend to Narnia' because, as she grows up, 'She's interested in nothing now-a-days except nylons and lipstick and invitations' (Lewis [1956] 1994, 169).

Miller may have experienced a growing distance between herself and the book's ideology but her relationship with Narnia persisted, 'as rocky as any love affair, a story of enchantment, betrayal, estrangement, and reunion' (Miller 2008, 3). In *The Magician's Book*, Miller explores ways in which the *Narnia* books can indeed be productively and pleasurably read by sceptics and unbelievers. A character like Lucy Pevensie offers a model of courage and candour; Edmund's betrayal gives us a complex example of moral seduction and avarice; the book's talking animals are the denizens of an appealingly enchanted world. *The Magician's Book* is also the story of the discovery of a community of readers, perhaps beginning with the elementary school teacher who first places the book in Miller's hands. In a quest to get a full understanding of what the series meant to its readers, Miller discusses the book with those who share Lewis's Christianity, representing a multitude of readers through the decades who have embraced the book's expression of faith. She talks to those even more sceptical than she is, most notably Philip Pullman, author of the *His Dark Materials* series, who is a vocal critic of the *Narnia* series, objecting to their Christian moralizing among other elements.

Like many memoirs of childhood reading, Miller captures the feeling of being enchanted by a children's book. But her study also reveals a persistent gulf between child and adult readers. For Miller, this gulf is experienced through her childhood ignorance of the book's motivating Christian symbolism. She also offers a narrative of the shattering of that ignorance; as an older child she felt rage about the kinds of lessons that adults were inviting her to learn. Above all, she offers us a narrative of trying to recapture that peculiar intensity of the nine-year-old 'who wants a place I've read about in a book to really exist' and a sense of reckoning with one's own literary past.

A similar intensity animates a series which is *not* for children, but that asks questions about the role of childhood reading as the specific province of childhood: Lev Grossman's *The Magicians Trilogy* (2009–2014), described by many as a kind of Harry Potter for grown-ups. Grossman's protagonist, Quentin Coldwater, is a depressed Brooklynite who broods obsessively over his childhood fantasy novels, set in a Narnia-like world named Fillory. When he is suddenly admitted to Brakebills College for Magical Pedagogy he discovers his affiliations with a magic community but struggles with its complexities. His wonderment when Fillory proves to be real gives way to despair when it turns out to be not the innocuous, benign place of his imagination but wild and frightening. Throughout the series Quentin's moral blind spots and weakness of character, especially in his relationships with women, are partially rooted in his continued fixation on the Fillory books and his inability to 'grow up.' Childhood reading, rather than leading to maturation, makes maturation difficult.

The very idea of children's literature presumes that children require a literature all their own: designed and made for them. But this presumption raises a number of questions, both definitional and cultural. Before children's literature as a category can emerge, do we need to have a modern concept of childhood? How do we deal with the many texts read by children that seem to fall outside the boundaries of children's literature? If we presume that children's literature is the literature meant for children, how do we account for enthusiastic adult readers of this literature? Should the boundaries of children's literature be defined, and what do we lose or gain by doing so?

Children's literature is, in fact, one of the few types of literature defined by the age group of its presumed audience. Most definitions of children's literature have, in fact, taken it as a given that children's literature is produced *for* children by adults, although recent critics have granted increased attention to children as cultural and literary producers, including their own books and digital **fan fiction**: written works that fans produce themselves as responses to an original text. These are often unauthorized, and most often not published professionally. As Richard Flynn notes, 'Children are also capable of creatively misappropriating the cultural artifacts they inherit from adults and transforming them into their own texts.' Recognizing this, increasing numbers of scholars strive to 'respect children's subjectivities and take them seriously' (Flynn 2011, 66).

Some of the most exciting recent scholarship in Children's Literature has focused attention on the roles of race, gender, sexuality, and social class in constructing childhood. What has shifted most in the light of this kind of scrutiny is the idea of a universally protected childhood and a literature that shares the assumptions that children must be taught, but at the same time shielded from, many adult realities. Work on race, gender, disability, and social class serves as a means to pierce the idealization of childhood, as scholars reckon with the ways in which childhood is not always a sheltered and cherished space but one where children face similar challenges to their adult counterparts, with their literature reflecting those challenges.

Complicating questions of definition is the fact that 'children's literature' refers both to a subset of literary works and to a field of academic study. As an academic field, it draws from several disciplines including (but not limited to) literary study, education, developmental psychology, and librarianship. Children's Literature can be studied both within a single discipline's methodologies and parameters, or it can take an interdisciplinary form and draw on several methodologies. Peter Hunt laments the lack of consensus in Children's Literature as a field:

> There are many thousands of undergraduate and graduate degrees called 'children's literature' across the world, although in practice many have little in common. They range from primary education to abstract theory, and from aspects of childhood studies to the most arcane bibliography, and despite a common title, they do not present a coherent, or even mutually comprehensible core (Hunt 2011, 47).

In this book I do not presume that methodological difference forecloses communication. Instead, and especially in Chapters 4 and 5, I will consider how the conscious acknowledgement of methodological differences can add to our understanding of children's literature. A researcher from one discipline might stress an aspect of the text and reception ignored within another discipline; the result will be an enhancement of critical understanding. Also, some of the most dynamic work in the field seeks to erode methodological boundaries, sometimes in startling ways.

As a field of study, Children's Literature has observed a traditional distinction between 'book people' and 'child people.' 'Book people' differentiate their work from the methodologies of librarianship and education, usually with the hope of shoring up the legitimacy of children's literature criticism within literary studies; especially in the 1970s and 1980s, when children's literature was finding a place within literary studies. 'Child people,' in contrast, work with actual children to understand literacy acquisition, book selection, and reception. Yet scholars of Children's Literature are challenging the boundaries between 'book people' and 'child people' and asking whether this division is productive or even legitimate. Flynn puts this most forcefully: 'If being a book person means promoting meaningful rather than merely functional literacy, then book people are child people indeed' (Flynn 1997, 145).

Margaret Mackey's *One Child Reading: My Auto-Bibliography* (2016) works to bring together critical engagement and personal experience, and to combine disciplines such as psychology, education, history, and literary studies. In *One Child Reading*, Mackey considers her own emerging literacies in Newfoundland, Canada, in the 1950s by examining the physical geography of her childhood (her room, her neighbourhood); the singular politics and demographics of her hometown and province; and the cultural institutions that supported her early reading and sense-making, from schools to churches to museums. *One Child Reading* follows from her earlier article, 'Reading from the Feet Up' (2010), which argued that children learn to read at the same time as they are beginning to explore their physical environment: both reading and physical exploration involve mapping and schema-making. Granted, a good portion of *One Child Reading*—which spans some 600 pages—is devoted to chronicling what Mackey cannot know about her early development, including an inability to access the memories of earliest infancy, which, following novelist Wayne Johnston, she describes as 'the Murk': a time before conscious understanding (Mackey 2016, 106). Mackay is keenly aware that she is offering only *one child's* account. Her book is likely to resonate primarily with Mackey's Baby Boom generation, especially women who recognize some of the cultural products aimed at girl readers in the 1950s. Yet, by virtue of its comprehensive look at childhood reading, it reveals the social, political, geographical, and familial factors that shape anyone's attainment of literacy.

Children's Literature scholars have been compelled to think about issues of audience and authorship that have sometimes been taken for granted in other areas of literary study, and to theorize the nature of its intended readership in complex ways. The popularity of young adult texts like *Harry Potter* or *Divergent* or *The Hunger Games* with adult readers has caused many to question whether categories such as 'children's literature' or 'young adult literature' are really meaningful. **Age levelling**, the sorting of books into age-appropriate categories such as 'Ages 5–9' or grades such as 'Middle Grade,' is a useful tool for the selection of books, but if followed too strictly might discourage individual readers from exploring books they might enjoy even if they are deemed 'too easy' or 'too difficult' for their age group.

The New Critical Idiom: Children's Literature will begin by exploring some of the competing definitions that animate the field, with a particular emphasis on what is excluded. The boundaries of Children's Literature as a field continue to be redrawn and challenged, sometimes dramatically. In Chapter 2, I engage with how scholarship on earlier periods (such as medieval and early modern) and on global children's literatures offers fresh perspectives on the history of children's literature. Chapter 3 is devoted to the question of politically committed children's literature, noting that children's literature has long been conceived of as instilling political, social, or religious belief in its young readers. Chapter 4 will look at new critical approaches to children's literature, including cognitive approaches, **Childhood Studies**, and new work in race, gender, and sexuality. Chapter 5 is devoted to questions of how works for children engage with some of the 21st century's greatest challenges, including global justice, ecological challenges, and the fraught relationships between people and animals, drawing on new thinking about **postcolonial** theory, **ecocriticism**, and **animal studies**.

1
DEFINITIONS

Definers and anti-definers

Roderick McGillis once called the energy scholars put into defining children's literature 'a mug's game' that 'deflects them from confronting important issues such as the subversive potential or the political implications of their subject' (McGillis 2009, 261). Marah Gubar notes the virtues of keeping definitions of children's literature as open as possible:

> The fact that something is very difficult to define—even 'impossible to define exactly'—does not mean that it does not exist or cannot be talked about. In such cases, we simply have to accept that the concept under consideration is complex and capacious; it may also be unstable (its meaning shifts over time and across different cultures) and fuzzy at the edges (its boundaries are not fixed and exact). Childhood is one such concept; children's literature is another (Gubar 2011, 212).

For Gubar, the lack of consensus is 'no real impediment' for 'the vast, silent majority of scholars' who 'cheerfully carry on with their scholarship on specific texts, types, and eras of children's literature' (Gubar 2011, 210).

Overly firm definitions prevent us from exploring texts that might enrich our understanding of children's literature. This includes texts that may have been part of the outlook of children in an earlier generation but are not read now, and texts not intended for children but enjoyed and read by them nevertheless. Many definitions of children's literature that stressed qualities of simplicity of form and theme, Gubar notes, had the effect of excluding many authors from children's literature's '**golden age**' in the late 19th and early 20th centuries, a time that produced many of the works that are now considered 'classics.' Works such as Tom Hood's *From Nowhere to the North Pole* (1875), with its quicksilver reversals between the human and the animal worlds, exhibited both sly humour and a strong current of satire, and can therefore fall between the cracks of a definition that stresses simplicity of form and theme.

Too much adherence to strict definitions, then, runs the risk of narrowing a critic's field of vision. Gubar, for one, would prefer that we err on the side of inclusion. There is no doubt that some critics espouse an 'anti-definer' stance out of frustration that a definition of children's literature remains elusive. This is well expressed in John Rowe Townsend's remark: 'Since any line-drawing must be arbitrary, one is tempted to abandon the attempt and say there is no such thing as children's literature, there is just literature. And in an important sense, that is true. Children are not a separate form of life from people; no more than children's books are a separate form of literature from just books' (Townsend 1980, 196–197). Townsend's argument, while in many ways appealing, fails to account for any qualities of children's literature that make it distinct from adult literature.

Perry Nodelman, staunchly positioned in the 'definer's camp,' contends that many people refuse to define children's literature because they have an almost mystical sense of childhood's ineffability: 'Childhood cannot be defined because definition is an act of logic and reason, and childhood is presumably the antithesis of logic and reason—a time of innocence, the glory of which is exactly its irrationality, the lack of knowledge and understanding that presumably offers insight into a greater wisdom' (Nodelman 2008, 147). Ironically, he asserts, those who resist pinning down a definition of childhood actually hold a firm definition of it as 'a form of pastoral or utopian idyll' (Nodelman 2008, 147). He believes that all works of children's literature share elements in common and that there is a need to identify their common features. His own list spans four pages of bullet points with 45 distinct qualities that help him identify a text as a work of children's literature, including techniques such as 'a childlike view of the events described' (Nodelman 2008, 77).

Defining Children's Literature: shaping the field

While it is true that a vast number of Children's Literature scholars are able to proceed with their work even in the absence of definitional consensus, it is a rare Children's Literature scholar who has never reflected on the boundaries of their field or what distinguishes a work of children's literature. It is in that spirit that we will examine some of the prevailing definitions of children's literature, aware that each definition allows for a certain vision of children's literature but excludes others. As Gubar noted, definitions of children's literature shape our encounter with the texts themselves and what we exclude from our field of vision. But should the genre be defined by its formal qualities, the subjective experience of the readers, the intentions of its authors, the contours of the literary market, or some combination of these factors? I will explore various definitions, but I will also identify exceptions that render these definitions flawed or non-viable. What is clear, ultimately, is that social and political institutions determine the contours of children's literature and also determine our working definitions of children's literature.

When trying to isolate what makes children's literature distinct, critics frequently start with its formal qualities, especially the ostensible simplicity of children's books. Myles McDowell offered such a definition in 1973:

children's books are generally shorter; they tend to favour an active rather than a passive treatment, with dialogue and incident rather than description and introspection; child protagonists are the rule; conventions are much used; the story develops within a clear-cut moral schematism which much adult fiction ignores; children's books tend to be optimistic rather than depressive; language is child-oriented; plots are of a distinctive order, probability is often disregarded ... (McDowell 1973, 51).

Peter Hunt aptly notes that this is a 'circular definition' (Hunt 2011, 45). Children's literature is anything with a shorter, simpler structure; works with a shorter, simpler structure are children's literature. In addition to its circularity, we can question the individual characteristics McDowell assigns to children's literature. Even the supposedly clear-cut morality of C.S. Lewis's *Narnia* books, with their overt allegories of good and evil, has its ambiguities. Edmund's perfidy is attributed to the malign influence of his school, which makes the narrative more complicated and serves as something of an absolution of his wicked betrayals. Richard Adams' *Watership Down* (1972) presents another challenge to McDowell's sense of the simplicity of children's literature. Epic in length, with intertwined adventure, myth, and folklore, *Watership Down* draws self-consciously from classical epics by Homer and Virgil to tell the story of a warren of rabbits that escapes an environmental disaster to seek a new home. It also includes words from the rabbits' own invented language, and this vocabulary is essential for an understanding of the rabbits' culture. Finally, the work's themes are morally complex and require critical judgments from its readers. For example, at one point the main group of wild rabbits encounters a prosperous warren known as Cowslip's Warren, named after Cowslip, the first rabbit they meet. They soon discover that the tame rabbits are surrounded by human snares but ignore these threats to enjoy material comfort for a comfortable life, laying bare the theme of freedom and security. In its contrasting models of heroism, the book asks readers to make judgments about physical strength vs. intellectual acuity. *Watership Down* allows for darkness and pessimism, especially as regards the impact of human intervention in nature. It is very far away from the brevity and simplicity (both moral and formal) McDowell stresses, and helps us see the innate limitations of his definition. Some critics, to be sure, do challenge the classification of *Watership Down* as children's literature. But others read the book as central within the children's literature tradition, not to mention the many child readers who have read and enjoyed the book through the years.

In one of the first studies of children's literature, written in 1932, F.J. Harvey Darton offered a much-quoted definition of children's literature as 'printed books produced ostensibly to give children spontaneous pleasure, and not primarily to teach them, nor solely to make them good, nor to keep them *profitably* quiet' (Darton [1932] 1982, 1). This, of course, excludes much literature that is didactic in nature, and in particular some of the earliest children's literature. In Darton's definition, children's literature is specifically crafted to offer children diversion. As we will see in Chapter 2, this is often a position associated with the 19th century 'golden age' of children's literature, with the anti-didacticism of writers such as Lewis Carroll. It may even exclude works such as concept picture-books, which are widely produced today and which function to teach children the alphabet, their numbers, and so on. You could argue that these works, too, are capable of offering their young readers pleasure, with visually and verbally appealing elements and the not-inconsiderable delight of mastering concepts. Perhaps Darton's definition could apply to such works, but then the lines between the books 'meant to teach them' and those that offer 'spontaneous pleasure' become hopelessly muddled. Basing the definition of children's literature on its capacity to spark or sustain pleasure obviously raises problems; the notion of 'spontaneous pleasure' is too subjective to serve as a reliable sign of children's literature.

We might consider a definition based on children's ownership of their own books. This, of course, excludes those children who do not have the resources or the desire to own books but who still read. It also links children's literature with capitalist systems that encourage private ownership of goods and the cultivation of an ethic of ownership in youth. Many scholars have considered children's literature as a process of **embourgeoisement**, the inculcation of middle-class ideals. Yet a definition that pivots on children's ownership of their own books ignores the fact that a book read out loud to a child at a library or schoolroom is still children's literature, even if the book is not owned by the child or by the child's family.

Others base their understanding of children's literature on a specific understanding of private reading, as distinguished from an oral tradition. In his controversial *The Disappearance of Childhood*, Neil Postman ([1982] 1994) argued that institutions that promoted childhood literacy gave rise to the phenomenon of 'childhood,' complete with its own literature. Adults in their turn kept 'a rich content of secrets' from the young: 'secrets about sexual relations, but also about money, about violence, about illness, about death, about social relations (Postman [1982] 1994).' In his view, contemporary mass media culture has eroded the boundaries between child and adult: both childhood and children's literature disappear when children are exposed to the same mass media products consumed by adults. This concept of children's literature excludes dramatic productions shared by child and adult audiences and any book read aloud to a mixed audience of children and adults, especially in earlier periods in history. For example, Abigail Williams' (2017) *Social Life of Books: Reading Together in the Eighteenth-Century Home* talks about reading in 18th-century England as a collective and intergenerational practice that often involved books read aloud: a model of literacy that did not separate child and adult audiences, despite the presence of some bowdlerization.

When defining children's literature as the literature that adults write with a child audience in mind, we violate the often-stated *tabu* in literary criticism against the 'intentional fallacy,' the assumption that the meaning of a work is inherent in the intentions of the author. In 1946, W.K. Wimsatt and Monroe Beardsley wrote an essay challenging the notion that an author's intention can be discerned from a given literary work. Any explicit statements about the intended meaning of the work from the author or anyone else can be similarly misleading (Wimsatt and Beardsley 1946). Basing a definition of children's literature on the idea that it is the literature *intended* for children, therefore, does not account for the ways in which children have claimed many books never intended for them. On the other hand, Linda Hutcheon offers a subtle critique of the intentional fallacy, noting that New Critics such as Wimsatt and Beardsley (as well as poststructuralist critics such as Roland Barthes and Michel Foucault) objected to the use of 'authorial intent as the *sole* arbiter and guarantee of the meaning and value of a work of art. No one denies that creative artists have intentions; the disagreements have been over how those intentions should be deployed in the interpretation of meaning and the assignment of value' (Hutcheon and O'Flynn 2013, 106–107). There is still, then, some value in exploring the author's intention. It still matters. For example, Enid Blyton and J.K. Rowling wrote for children intentionally. Sue Townsend's *The Secret Diary of Adrian Mole, Aged 13¾* (1982) is written in the voice of a teenager, but much of its delicious irony is aimed at an adult readership, as was her intention.

Some critics see children's literature as encompassing anything at all that children read, including works clearly intended for adults, with the understanding that anything read by a child is 'children's literature.' This is a definition respectful of the range of children's reading and willing to acknowledge how wide in scope it can be. However, if anything, this definition is too capacious and does not go very far in delineating the boundaries of children's literature, since in theory any literary work could be included. If Gubar is right to argue that we should avoid a definition that is too narrow, some might argue that we should avoid a definition that is too broad.

Barbara Wall roots the definition of children's literature in the tonal and narrative changes that happen when adults write for children:

> My conclusions are founded on the conviction that adults, whether or not they are speaking ironically, speak differently in fiction when they are aware that they are addressing children. Such subtleties of address define a children's book (Wall 1991).

Many critics have developed an understanding of children's literature as a mixture of younger and older voices, and one that speaks to children and adults simultaneously. U.C.

Knoepflmacher and Mitzi Myers introduced the concept of 'cross-writing,' noting that 'a dialogic mix of older and younger voices occurs in texts too often read as univocal. Authors who write for children inevitably create a colloquy between past and present selves' (Knoepflmacher and Myers 1997, vii).

Some definitions of children's literature are based on the notion that it is the literature that best captures the physical, psychological, or existential experience of childhood. Peter Hollindale, for example, notes in his *Signs of Childness in Children's Books* (1997) that '**childness** is the distinguishing property of a text in children's literature, setting it apart from other literature as a genre, and it is also the property that the child brings to the reading of a text' (Hollindale 1997, 47). Hollindale reads children's literature as a place where many interests meet:

> the children's concern with the presentness of her own childhood, and interest in its possibilities; the adult's recall of childhood and desire to refresh the roots and keep a sense of continuous identity; and the adult's hopes and beliefs and desires about childhood, what it is and what it ought to be (Hollindale 1997, 42).

Here we see children's literature fulfilling a range of wishes and needs for very different readers. As Kimberley Reynolds explains: 'Hollindale proposes that children's books create a space where adulthood and childhood can meet and mingle, with adults reactivating aspects of what it was like to be a child—particularly the mutability and potentiality of childhood—while children gain insights into what it is like to be adult' (Reynolds 2011, 55). While children seek adult knowledge, adults, in contrast, seek to connect with their own childhood, constructed in imagination as a simpler and more pleasurable time. Maria Nikolajeva describes children's literature (distinguishing it from young adult literature) as 'optative' or presenting a utopian vision of childhood that reflects the realm of childhood as adults want it to be, 'not as it is, but as adult authors remember it, as they wish it were or had been and might be in the future, and not least what they wish, consciously or subconsciously, that young readers should believe it is' (Nikolajeva

2014, 33). When encountering content that seems to puncture that innocence, adult readers express a sense of shock, wanting to shield children from the seamier side of life, a desire that many child readers in their eagerness to attain worldly knowledge do not share.

For Nodelman, children's literature aspires to control its child readers by underscoring the polarities between adult and child, often in complicated ways. Behind every work of children's literature there is a phenomenon he terms the 'hidden adult,' a sophisticated adult knowledge that remains in seemingly innocent texts for children. In a perceptive review of *The Hidden Adult,* McGillis notes:

> Adults desire both to end innocence and to preserve it. Such ambiguities necessarily find their way into books for children. And so all books for young readers present their child readers with a world that is simple enough for them to grasp, but this very simplicity implies a condition that is not simple (McGillis 2009, 257).

In Nodelman's model, children often learn from children's literature how to be childlike, or how to perform a childlike naïveté that is appealing to adults. I will return later in this chapter to the polarities between adult writer and child reader that have animated so much of the theorization of children's literature.

Other polarities have affected the development and definition of children's literature, including gender differences. M.O. Grenby provocatively asks: 'Is there such a thing as children's literature in any case? Might it be more accurate to talk of a boys' literature and a girls' literature?' (Grenby 2008, 8). Gender difference, then, is one of many possible differences in the child audience (or of any audience) that make it impossible to generalize about children's literature as a body. Much of children's literature, if not all of it, is tailored to a certain demographic group. In Chapter 4, for example, we will see that differences between children (including gender, race, class, sexuality, or any combination of these differences) are driving the articulation of new literary histories and new definitions of the field.

In summary, rooting a definition of children's literature in formal qualities fails, because counter-examples can always be found. Nor can it be rooted in any one experience of book ownership, or children as recipients of a literature crafted for them. Conflicting accounts of the definition, social purpose, and formal qualities of children's literature may give the impression that we will never get close to defining the field or come to grips with its cultural meaning. But that might send us back to looking more specifically at each work, seeing how it functions within its own composition, distribution, and reception histories. Furthermore, the ongoing debates about the definition of 'children's literature' reveal different facets of what children's literature is and how it functions culturally.

Including and excluding texts in the genre

How can you tell when a book is explicitly *not* for children? Answering this question might help us move to a definition of children's literature, since it reveals the immense energy our culture expends on what is appropriate for children and what is beyond the pale. We see this in the fact that so many censorship challenges pivot around children's texts as adults object to their children reading certain texts that do not accord with their sense of what children *should* read. Children's literature is seen as a necessary part of a child's development; many stakeholders in that process are willing to invest a great deal of energy and thought in what young people read. Put less positively, it can be read as a market that commodifies childhood and reduces children and their caregivers to consumers.

Limit cases that challenge the boundaries of children's literature are illuminating. Profanity, sexuality, and violence are often thought to be inappropriate for children, and even for young adults. Nodelman argues that the range of 'excludable texts and properties within texts' is 'wide and various':

> books adults think children won't like, books adults think children will like but shouldn't, nonchildist books or nonquality books, books with language too complex for children's limited cognitive abilities, texts

too long for children's limited attention spans, material too violent for children's tender sensibilities or too sexy for children's innocent purity—or, alternatively, material violent enough or sexy enough to dangerously arouse children's uncontrollable passions (Nodelman 2008, 152).

According to this model, the field of children's literature is a negotiation between what is culturally permitted and what is culturally forbidden. Nodelman notes the horrified reactions of early reviewers to Maurice Sendak's *Where the Wild Things Are* (1963), despite the charm of the Wild Things and the mischievous twinkles in their eyes, although these reviewers were forgetting longstanding traditions of fairy tale monsters or figures such as Shock-Headed Peter (Nodelman 2008, 121). After *Where the Wild Things Are*, monsters in children's literature were more accepted. Nodelman, however, notes that there are limits to the kinds of monsters who might appear in children's literature. Forbidden characters might include

> monsters made of human feces come to life, perhaps, or monsters who made children happy by fondling their privates or who encouraged children to brush their teeth every day and to refuse all candy and then turned out to be evil and wrong (Nodelman 2008, 123).

It is hard to argue with this. Such outré monsters will probably never feature in books for children. The boundaries of what is acceptable for children are set both by prevailing cultural norms and the politics and dynamics of the publishing industry. For Nodelman, a work of children's literature might push at the boundaries of the field but never fully break them. On the other hand, historical examples like *Struwwelpeter* (*Shock-Headed Peter*) challenge Nodelman's sense of the unthinkable in children's literature. A contemporary publisher would almost certainly not produce a book that depicts graphic punishments for child misbehaviour, such as a girl who is burned to death when she plays with matches or a boy who has his hands cut off with scissors because he sucks his thumb. Children in the past read (and possibly enjoyed) such books, as well as nursery rhymes like

'Alouette,' where a speaker threatens to pluck the feathers from a lark in retribution for being woken up by its song. It is also undeniably true that children's literature throughout its history has contained elements of the scatological or bawdy humour of various kinds. As one of innumerable examples, Roald Dahl's *The BFG* (1982) features the title character of the Big Friendly Giant who drinks frobscottle, whose bubbles go downwards and cause noisy flatulence called 'whizzpoppers.'

A more recent text that pushes the boundaries of children's literature is Elena Ferrante's recently translated picture-book *The Beach at Night*. First published (without controversy) in Italy in 2007, it appeared translated in English and illustrated by Mara Cerri in 2016. It is the story of Celina, a doll who spends a night of terror and abandonment on the beach when Mati—a little girl to whom she is devoted—accidentally leaves her there. The Mean Beach Attendant sings a cruel and profane song when raking the beach and threatens to steal all of Celina's words. She is threatened by fire, borne away by a storm, and submerged in the ocean. Although Celina is rescued by the cat Minù and brought back to her little girl, the book's undertones of rape and abjection were felt by American reviewers to be pushing the boundaries. The *New York Times* review wryly points to cultural differences:

> In Europe, darker picture books are common. Presumably just as the children of Europe willingly eat escargots and tripe stew at dinnertime, they fall asleep to picture books with titles like 'My First Nightmare' and 'A Visit from Death' (Russo 2016).

Whether the children of Europe are made of sterner stuff than their American counterparts must remain an open question. But it is clear that there are different norms within the publishing industry itself; the American publisher classified the audiobook (read by Natalie Portman) as a book for adults. Much depends, apparently, on the translation of the Mean Beach Attendant's expletives when he tells Celina he has 'shit' for her 'craw.' In Italian, this word might be translated as 'poo' rather than 'shit.' It seems like the boundaries between children's and adult literature are almost experienced as arbitrary standards rather than as a set of core traits in the book, sometimes as subtle as the tonal differences between a word like 'poo' and one like 'shit.'

As we saw earlier, our definitions of children's literature are bound up with notions of childhood innocence, but there is debate about whether that innocence even applies to current childhood and whether a literature that preserves that innocence is warranted. Julia L. Mickenberg and Lynne Vallone, in their introduction to the *Oxford Handbook of Children's Literature*, argue that the distinctions between literature for adults and that for children are increasingly blurred:

> in the contemporary moment we seem to be at a point where the lines dividing children's literature and literature for adults often cannot be easily drawn, which may come down to the fact that without 'innocence' as a clear demarcation of the line between childhood and adulthood, we are losing a sense of that boundary as well as the need for it (Mickenberg and Vallone 2011, 17).

Perry Nodelman disagrees:

> In what I myself see as a time of increasingly repressive surveillance of and protectiveness toward children and of ongoing commodification of the cuteness of childhood innocence in the marketplace, the unconvincing assertion that we are moving beyond our cultural commitment to the idea of childhood as a safe preserve comes across as yet another way in which [current reference works in the field of children's literature] are attempting to downplay the connections between children's literature, children, and childhood (Nodelman 2013, 156).

Nodelman is quite willing, he notes, to acknowledge the diversity and complexity of 'actual children' (Nodelman 2013, 154), but he is firm in his belief that children's literature itself emerges from the cultural desire to assert and preserve childhood innocence.

The questions of whether children's literature can be defined as a literature that addresses the specific psychological, social, and cultural needs of children as a protected and innocent class frequently widen when looking outside the Anglo-American world. For example, Ann González, in *Resistance and Survival: Children's*

Narrative from Central America and the Caribbean (2009), considers questions of knowingness in the region's children's literature. The many **trickster figures** animating Central American and Caribbean literature do not resemble the 'underdog' of North American or European children's literature but serve as figures of survival and resistance:

> While U.S. and European literatures train their children to become better members of the dominant class (Kutzer), Latin American children, who have a long history of domination, first by Spain and then by the United States, have other lessons to learn: for example, how to resist submission or submit with dignity; how to fight the odds and insist on cultural, if not political, independence; how to get what they want without appearing to do so or without angering the dominant class; how to speak through silence and have the last laugh (González 2009, 1)

Trickster figures 'find ways to cover their tracks and hide what they do; they speak on multiple, sometimes even contradictory, levels to multiple audiences: children, adults, colleagues, and peers. Yet the message is always fundamentally the same: how to get what is necessary without direct confrontation or open resistance' (González 2009, 8). To consider the cultural functions of a children's literature which stresses savvy resistance, we might turn to a picture-book by Chilean writer Antonio Skármeta and illustrated by Alfonso Ruano: *The Composition* (2000). *The Composition* features Pedro, a young boy who lives in an unnamed country under an authoritarian regime and who has seen his parents' friends suddenly disappear. Military officials, seeing children as sources of information about the political resistance of their families, come to Pedro's school to announce a prize for the best paper on the theme 'What My Family Does at Night.' Although Pedro's parents are in fact members of the resistance who spend their nights listening to the radio for news, he writes that his parents play chess at night. When he reveals the subject of his composition to his parents, his father notes with relief and wry irony: 'I guess we'll have to buy a chess set' (Skármeta 2000, n.p.). Although early in the book Pedro's parents tell him that children should not concern themselves with politics, he proves them wrong. As Niall Nance-Carroll remarks: 'Pedro's successful deception represents a victory for his family, but it also represents in part a child's victory over his parents, who have attempted to convince him that childhood is a state without political views, acts, or responsibilities' (Nance-Carroll 2014, 276). One way to expand our vision of children's literature, then, is to look at it within an international context in order to see what roles specific political structures play. Local, regional, and national specificities affect children's experiences and shape their literature.

Emer O'Sullivan points to the ways in which the definition of children's literature is political in exactly this sense, and that it cannot be determined 'on the level of the text itself, that is to say in the form of specific textual features.' For O'Sullivan, determinations of what is suitable for young people are made by 'social authorities,' which include 'educational institutions both ecclesiastical and secular, figures active in the literary market (publishers, distributers, etc.) and those who produce the books (editors, authors, etc.)' (O'Sullivan 2005a, 12). In this formulation, children's literature is the product of many actors and a combination of institutions and individuals. As the complex interrelations between institutions and individuals change, so will the very nature of literature for children. Here O'Sullivan gets close to a definition of children's literature, not by stressing its core features but by acknowledging it as a product of institutional values intersecting with individual experience. Such a method of thinking about children's literature allows for infinite variance, and even contradictory values and qualities, and requires a full understanding of where a work falls within its multiple literary and cultural histories. This is well expressed by Jack Zipes:

> For a children's book to be recognized as a book *for* children, a system had to be in place. That is, a process of production, distribution, and reception had to be instituted within which places were assigned to different groups of people. Gender, age, and social class played roles. Indeed, it was not possible for a broad range of books to be approved and to reach children in specific ways until the system of production, distribution, and reception was instituted and became focused on how to socialize children through reading (Zipes 2001, 46).

Ultimately, the Children's Literature scholar needs to ask incisive questions about the 'ownership' of children's literature. As Peter Hollindale asks:

> if the literature is owned by children, is it therefore not owned by adults? In meeting the needs of an immature audience, does it inevitably omit the necessary interests of a mature one? In order to read it, must we disrobe ourselves of our maturity, at least in part, in order to read as a child reads? Are we unavoidably stepping back, whether in nostalgia or condescension or escape, in order to reoccupy a prior self? Is it indeed possible to do this? (Hollindale 1997, 8–9).

Hollindale's questions are all the more effective because he acknowledges that children construct childhood as they go along. Complicating this issue is the fact that children's literature has the potential to follow us through an entire life cycle. For example, Laura Miller's transmuted but never fully ruptured relationship with C.S. Lewis's *The Lion, The Witch and the Wardrobe* reveals both a text that changes as people change, and a melancholic inability to recapture an earlier childhood reading.

Adult authors, child readers

Children's literature is one of the few literary forms to be defined by the age, or more specifically the life stage, of its intended audience. Apart from some notable instances of child authorship and juvenile production (such as Gordon Korman's raucous 1978 school story *This Can't Be Happening at Macdonald Hall*), it is written by adults. To define children's literature—to establish its contours, limits, and nature—is inevitably to grapple with this asymmetry in some way. Dynamics of power, autonomy, and authority vary widely between individuals and groups, to be certain, but, in the aggregate, children lack the material and cultural resources available to adults, they do not enjoy the same levels of independence, and they lack the same worldly experience. In *The Case of Peter Pan, or the Impossibility of Children's Fiction* (1984), Jacqueline Rose forcefully engaged with this asymmetry brought about by adults writing literature for children: 'There is, in one sense, no body of literature which rests so openly on an acknowledged difference, a rupture almost, between writer and addressee. Children's fiction sets up the child as an outsider to its own process, and then aims, unashamedly, to take the child *in*' (Rose [1984] 1992, 2). In referring to the 'impossibility' of children's literature in her subtitle, Rose was not in fact arguing that books like *Peter Pan* or *Charlotte's Web* do not actually *exist*. She was asserting that books such as *Peter Pan* are produced for adult needs rather than those of children: a repository for adult hopes, anxieties, and fantasies. Following Freud and Lacan, Rose contended that adults producing children's literature have an innate investment in a notion of the child whose development was linear. To Rose, the writer of children's literature and the institutions that promote and disseminate children's literature have a vision of the child as a stable point of origin. Above all, adults had an investment in a childhood innocence that children's literature was meant to promote, protect, and embody. Hence children's literature involved a great deal of manipulation and involved a wholesale projection of adult values on to children.

Rose's work had an enormous impact on the field; it was a much-needed corrective to assumptions that children's literature could speak in a simple and direct way to its readers. David Rudd and Anthony Pavlik note its timeliness in an institutional sense as well, since it offered Children's Literature legitimacy in English and Literature departments: 'the emerging academic study of children's literature was trying to find its theoretical feet within an area that, while often celebrating the aesthetic and literary qualities of texts, had tended toward the utilitarian' (Rudd and Pavlik 2010, 223). Rose inspired literary critics in particular to try to cultivate some scepticism about children's literature's connection with its young readers.

Critics of Rose objected, and still object, to her stress on asymmetrical power relationships, arguing for the ways in which children's literature from the 19th century onward was attuned to child pleasures and desires, and moments where children collaborated with adults to shape the production of children's literature. Others are less convinced of the absolute gap between children and adults. Rudd has been eloquent on this point, noting 'children's fiction is only really impossible if we see children as distinct from adults, standing outside society and language, rather than being actively involved in negotiating meaning' (Rudd 2010, 290–291). Rudd turns to the ideas of Mikhail Bahktin and Valentin Vološinov to explore **dialogism**:

> we, from our own particular historical and social location, are forever in dialogue with the texts we encounter (for example, as a child, female, middle class, Northerner, fan of science fiction, or whatever); and ... these different discursive affiliations interact with a text that is itself made up of different discursive elements. To use the Russians' terminology, albeit in translation, a text has "multi-accentuality" (Vološinov) or "heteroglossia" (Bakhtin *Dialogic [Imagination]*), such that a work is always dynamic, always subject to struggles over its signification. In this model, children's fiction is always and forever possible, though its effectiveness can never be fully gauged (Rudd 2010, 294–295).

Bakhtinian models of language underscore the idea that exchange and communication is possible even across significant difference. While Rudd is right to note that the effectiveness of children's fiction 'can never be fully gauged,' there is a recent effervescence of interest in children's participation in literary and cultural forms, which includes but is not limited to child authors. Gubar has developed something known as the **kinship model**:

> This model is premised on the idea that children and adults are akin to one another, which means they are neither exactly the same nor radically dissimilar. The concept of kinship indicates relatedness, connection, and similarity without implying homogeneity, uniformity, and equality (Gubar 2013, 453).

The 'kinship model' helps bridge the gaps between child and adult readers while not eliding the differences between them.

Childist criticism

In 1991 Peter Hunt argued for what he called a '**childist criticism**,' aimed at 'reading, as far as possible, from a child's point of view, taking into account personal, sub-cultural, experiential, and psychological differences between children and adults' (Hunt 1991, 198). While this is a laudable aim, it has inbuilt limitations, as our discussion so far should indicate, acknowledged in the qualifier 'as far as possible.' One way, however, in which a childist criticism can work is to centralize children's own literary opinions and preferences. Aidan Chambers, himself an established children's and YA novelist, developed a 'tell me' method where he outlines a means to get children to talk about books in an informed way and to support their observations with evidence. He notes: 'We begin to listen more attentively to the questions children generate themselves—and use those as springboards' (Chambers 1996, 85).

Much of the best criticism in this vein is distinguished by awareness of its own limitations, as we see from Hugh Crago's remarks on his own study of his daughter's reading:

> *observed response to literature is not equivalent to internal experience of literature....* All we can trace, measure, analyze, is what individuals *show* us of their experience through speech, facial expression, or gesture (Crago 1985, 101).

It is impossible for any individual to communicate the whole essence of their experience as a reader; those communications are also altered by the dynamics between the interlocutor and the respondent. This, however, is not unique to child readers, since all people possess different abilities and inhabit different circumstances. Those differences always need to be bridged when talking about books, appraising their impact, or working within the field of literary culture in general.

Childhood experience and children's literature

Jacqueline Rose and her followers, as I have noted, saw the gulf between children and adults as an impassable one, noting that adults sought to construct a childhood that harmonized with their own vision of childhood needs but that, above all, actually fed adult needs and fantasies. Some critics have responded by asserting that adults, and particularly authors for children, can actually have some access to those childhood experiences and capture them in literary form. In *Feeling Like a Kid: Childhood and Children's Literature* (2006), Jerry Griswold draws on the work of Alison Lurie to note that 'the great writers for children know—and their stories speak of and reveal— what it feels like to be a kid' (Griswold 2006, 4). Certainly, a number of children's literature authors have explicitly stated that they seek to be in touch with their childhood selves when they write, or even that they have never left those selves behind. One example of many is Maurice Sendak's remarks to Nat Hentoff about making contact with the child within himself: 'I communicate with him—or try to—all the time … The pleasures I get as an adult are heightened by the fact that I experience them as a child at the same time' (Hentoff 1966, 42).

In contrast to Rose, Griswold does not see the endeavour of writing for children as rooted in nostalgia. Rather, a writer can capture embodied childhood experiences, with five recurrent patterns: 'snugness,' most often seen in the cosy cabins, homes, and dens in children's literature; 'scariness,' allowing a certain 'discomforting fun'; 'smallness,' manifested in miniature people or objects; 'lightness,' seen in the abundance of 'airborne characters'; and 'aliveness,' revealed in talking animals, living toys, and animations of nature (Griswold 2006, 1–2). Objections to Griswold's specific categories are quick to appear. For one thing, these qualities might be said to reflect a certain middle- or upper-class childhood, with its particular boundaries and protections and with access to certain spaces and pleasures. Roberta Seelinger Trites points to the arbitrariness of Griswold's categories when she offers additional themes such as 'fullness' (acknowledging scholarship on children's literature and food, eating, and hunger), 'zaniness' (acknowledging the long critical engagement with nonsense), as well as 'queerness,' 'slowness,' or 'parentlessness.' Griswold's model is not adequate to serve as a fully-fledged account of everything children's literature can do, and everything it is (Trites 2007a, 395–396). It does, however, gesture towards children's literature's evocation of certain spaces and sensations, and opens the door to thinking about them critically and imaginatively.

Maria Tatar's *Enchanted Hunters: The Power of Stories in Childhood* (2009) works in a similar vein to try to explore the nature of childhood reading. For example, Tatar writes about the appeal of horror and terror for child readers, and also about the role of sensory imagery in offering reading pleasure. She also considers the powerful cultural function of the bedtime story and rituals of routine reading. The patterns that Griswold and Tatar find offer a glimpse of the impact and experience of children's literature. Indeed, for all of their limitations they effectively break down the distance between adult and child that Rose seeks to pinpoint.

Reception memoirs

One resource for Children's Literature scholars as they seek to understand the role of children's literature in the lives of children is provided by memoirs of reading. In the Introduction to this book I considered Margaret Mackey's 'auto-bibliography,' *One Child Reading,* as an example of an interdisciplinary project that seeks to reconstruct childhood reading and the acquisition of literacy, even if that reconstruction is necessarily imperfect. Journalist and critic Laura Miller's book about C.S. Lewis's *Narnia* series also devotes much time to charting her rapturous first readings of these books, especially *The Lion, The Witch and The Wardrobe.* In the appendix to *Enchanted Hunters,* Maria Tatar collects excerpts from an enormous variety of childhood reading, from adults from the 18th century to the present, with much emphasis on the emotions stirred by childhood reading.

Historical work on reading can also help us expand the purview of the discipline by looking at readers and literacy accounts from previously marginalized or understudied groups, as Jamie Campbell Naidoo and Sarah Park Dahlen point out when they focus on 18th century slave narratives like that of Olaudah Equiano: 'The authors of the slave narratives typically began by writing about what it was like to be a child in bondage. Thus, in these narratives, we have the origins of textually represented African American child life' (Dahlen and Naidoo 2013, 35).

Reception memoirs can offer a glimpse of the literary culture of a single generation. Francis Spufford's *The Child that Books Built: A Life in Reading* (Spufford 2002), for example, covers the terrain of British childhood reading in the 1960s, with its ample consumption of now-classic books (by writers such as C.S. Lewis, Maurice Sendak, Lewis Carroll, and J.R.R. Tolkien) but also by some of the British authors most in vogue at that time, such as Leon Garfield, Jill Paton Walsh, Penelope Farmer, Peter Dickinson, and Alan Garner. It is obvious that these memoirs need to be read as carefully created works of art in their own right, with obvious selectivity and embellishment. Traditionally, autobiographical accounts and memoirs have in fact been counted as the *least* reliable of all sources. Susan Honeyman, among many others, considers the elusive nature of adult memory when it surfaces in both fiction and non-fiction: 'Childhood is whatever adults have lost and maybe never had ... How can any adult writer convincingly present such an inconsistent and imaginary position with any sense of authority?' (Honeyman 2005, 4). But the recollection of childhood reading does shows that the impression made by children's literature often endures over many decades and life changes, even without full access to the thoughts and feelings of childhood. First-person accounts of reading might be best approached not as reliable data but rather as traces of memory and emotion related to that reading.

Book history and correspondence

Another way to explore how children interacted with their reading material is to draw on book history and children's correspondence. Karen Sánchez-Eppler, for example, described the book-destroying habits of Emily Dickinson's young niece and nephew, details of which she discovered in an archive. This encounter, naturally, opens as many questions as it answers:

> What to make of this 'destruction of books?' What does the mere fact of scribbling and cutting tell us about the children's relation to print culture? Mattie colored the letters of her alphabet primer yellow, red, and blue. Does coloring adorn or deface these letters? (Sánchez-Eppler 2011, 153).

Sánchez-Eppler argues for an affective connection between the children and their books: 'For these affluent children of the next generation, marking up books seems to have become part and parcel of learning to care about them' (Sánchez-Eppler 2011, 153).

The letters to authors written by children offer another promising archive, albeit one that, once again, has its limits. *Peter Pan's Postbag* (1909) was a series of missives from fans of the main Peter Pan actress, Pauline Chase. In our time, many children wrote letters to Judy Blume, the author of frank middle-grade books that touched on maturation, sexual development, and complex family dynamics. These epistolary overtures presume a kind of intimacy with the author, or create it. Many authors, such as Blume, actually do respond to these inquiries. In a recent article about agency in children's literature, Sara L. Schwebel stresses that letters to authors can be constructed to win adult approval:

> Historical sources authored by young people are limited, particularly before the mid-nineteenth century and especially for young and very young children. While this is a problem shared by other historical subjects (the working class), there is an additional challenge in the case of children: the sources that are available, particularly from historical periods but also from the contemporary era, were created largely under the supervision of adults. Letters, school assignments, and even diaries were frequently read and approved by grown-ups. The context in which such sources were produced—in institutional settings of the school and home, for pedagogical and spiritual exercises, under the guidance of adults and with the earnestness of youth seeking approval—makes it especially difficult to tease out the ideas of child writers. (Schwebel 2016, 279).

These historical sources might tell us something about educational conventions or epistolary etiquette, but they do not reveal children's 'genuine ideas about the books they have read or the ways they have accepted or rejected the world views presented in their pages' (Schwebel 2016, 282).

At the same time, letters from children might be more viable as a source if those letters were written voluntarily, as Brian Rouleau observes when he describes early 20th century readers who wrote letters to authors of popular series books as '[a] coherent and highly self-aware subculture consisting of young readers invested in both the authors of their favorite books and the lives of characters created by those authors' (Rouleau 2016, 404). These child readers were, in his words, 'clearly convinced of their right, even their duty, to influence series fiction narratives' (Rouleau 2016, 404). Reader suggestions allowed the presses to become attuned to contemporary sensibilities. Of course, these children were also participating in a commercial system, and reading clubs and junior presses were 'free advertising in the form of word-of-mouth praise and local distribution networks concentrated in clubhouses, libraries, and schoolyards' (Rouleau 2016, 413).

Child-centred literary criticism has shifted its attention to new work on **fan fiction** and fan sites authored by children, as well as children's co-authorship with adults and children as authors. The digital age has offered new possibilities for this kind of engagement: the polar opposite of the model of the child as a mute receptacle for literary and cultural texts. In drawing on evidence from book history, personal accounts and letters, as well as from the observations of child readers in classroom and home settings, Children's Literature scholars work towards an understanding of literature's impact, also drawing on established methodologies from education, library science, and childhood studies.

Children's literature vs. young adult literature

In several ways the divide between childhood and adolescence, and the passage between these two states, is a revealing litmus test for what children's literature is. Where does children's literature end and young adult literature begin? Just as children's literature can be defined against its 'adult' counterparts, young adult literature often serves as a foil to children's literature, with an inclusion of elements such as sexuality and the critique of authority that are ostensibly absent from children's literature. Many people, for example, have noted the definite shift from the early novels in J.K. Rowling's *Harry Potter* series to the later books, with their growing complexity and length. The later books, arguably beginning with the fifth book, *Harry Potter and the Order of the Phoenix* (2003), grow progressively darker as the Hogwarts students fight Voldemort—even forming a student-led paramilitary group at one point to practise their defensive skills—and confront some of the turbulent emotions of the transition to adulthood. Should the earlier books in the series be described as children's fiction and the later books as young adult fiction? If so, where does the distinction lie? Is it formal, thematic, or rooted in reader response? This interpretive problem should remind us of the search for a definition for children's literature generally. It is, as always, easy to make counter-arguments that the earlier books in the series do not lack dark content, as in Harry's extreme abuse at the hands of the Dursleys (he lives in a closet under the stairs), or Ginny's feverish encounter with Tom Riddle's diary in *Harry Potter and the Chamber of Secrets* (1998).

Our conception of the qualities of young adult literature as a separate genre is bound up with cultural notions about adolescence. G. Stanley Hall famously identified adolescence in 1904 as a particular life stage, one identified with modernity. Adolescence is in many ways defined as a time of transition made possible in modernity because it offers more scope for self-exploration. However, acknowledging that modern adolescence stemmed from 'nineteenth century social and institutional changes,' John Neubauer notes that it could also be seen as predating modernity: 'identity crises of youth, generational conflicts, processes of maturation, and initiation rites were traditional themes of literature well before adolescence as we know it emerged' (Neubauer, 1992, 75). In the medieval and early modern periods, for example, young people would often leave their families and go to live and work with another family or individual as apprentices, sometimes learning a trade or learning how to manage a household. This experience was a moment of transition and of emerging independence away from a family of origin; it sparked a number of conduct books and guides aimed at this specific demographic.

Other critics identify other pivotal moments for the development of adolescence as a distinct life stage. For Mary Hilton and Maria Nikolajeva, the First World War was a turning point in generational self-definition; in the 1920s and 1930s 'a new young generation of writers began to depict the moral and spiritual crises of that disinherited era' (Hilton and Nikolajeva 2012, 5). The Second World War, they note, was also a catalyst for the expression of an adolescent culture. Anne Frank's diary had a genuine effect in opening up the horizons of an adolescent culture, combining its coming of age narrative with her exceptional circumstances as she hid from the Nazis in an Amsterdam attic (Hilton and Nikolajeva 2012, 6).

In the post-war period in North America, adolescents acquired more purchasing power than they had in the past, which allowed for the development of a 'teenage' popular culture. The emergence of rock and roll in the late 1940s and early 1950s is one example; it helped catalyse a youth culture through fashion, record purchases, jukeboxes, and TV programs. The best known young adult book of the immediate post-war period is 1951's *The Catcher in the Rye,* where a disaffected Holden Caulfield reflects with disgust on the 'phonies' of adult culture. Caulfield distinguishes himself both from young children and from adults.

Many critics identify young adult literature as primarily a marketing category: a perception that has only intensified with the recent blockbuster success of many Young Adult (YA) books. Karen Coats, however, draws our attention to the instability of these marketing categories, noting that a work such as Alice Sebold's *The Lovely Bones* (2002) was not written with the YA audience in mind, but was embraced by young readers. Furthermore, 'savvy marketers have tapped into the crossover phenomenon by creating alternate covers and trim sizes that correspond to consumer expectations to house the same texts' (Coats 2010, 322). The same book, then, is claimed as an 'adult' and a 'young adult' text, framing and defining it within two possible markets.

Michael Cart notes that 'young adults are beings in evolution, in search of self and identity; beings who are constantly growing and changing, morphing from the condition of childhood to that of adulthood' (Cart 2008). Roberta Seelinger Trites, in *Twain, Alcott, and the Birth of the Adolescent Reform Novel* (2007), links that growth to political development, noting that 'these texts create a parallel between the individual's need to grow and the society's need to improve itself. In focusing on the growth of an individual character, we often miss the metaphorical use to which the individual's growth has been put' (Trites 2007b, 144). It certainly seems that there is a hunger for such narratives of growth. Julie Beck, responding in 2014 to a series of articles in the popular press that castigated adult readers for reading young adult fiction, argues that young adult literature is well suited to reflect times of growth or rapid change:

> what unites works of YA fiction, whether set on suburban streets or on a spaceship in the future, is how quickly and how dramatically its characters experience change ... narratives of change always resonate, even if, as adults, our own changes often happen more subtly (Beck, 2014).

The process of sexual maturation is seen as a definitive marker within YA literature, reflecting the experience of puberty as a phase of adolescent development. Some critics argue that the presence of sexual content means a book is a YA book and not a children's book; others do not see the inclusion of sexuality as the dividing line.

Young adult literature has become a cultural space not only for the developmental narratives so central to the genre, but also a cultural location for engaging contemporary political issues, among them cloning, environmental degradation, inequality, and gender. We see these conversations unfolding in both realistic fiction and fiction that is variously described as speculative or fantastic, including YA dystopias. This is not to say that children's literature does not tackle such subjects; we will see in Chapter 3 that literature for even the youngest children sometimes tackles sophisticated political ideas. But there seems to be a particular energy now in presenting these debates and issues to contemporary adolescent audiences or, at a minimum, a cultural appetite for presenting these conversations in the accessible form of YA literature. Hilton and Nikolajeva argue that YA literature marks 'the adolescent's struggle for fully adult capability and identity in areas that do in fact mark the teenager off from the child: in firstly *political* and in secondly *sexual* agency and awareness' (Hilton and Nikolajeva 2012, 11). Trites, in her landmark study of YA literature, *Disturbing the Universe: Power and Repression in Adolescent Literature* (Trites 2004), puts questions of power at the absolute centre of the genre: the exposure of authoritarian structures and the adolescent's own navigation of social structures work together in adolescent fiction.

The recent development of the 'emerging adult' category and what is often called 'New Adult fiction' has complicated matters of these age-levelled boundaries still further. Molly Wetta defines New Adult fiction as featuring protagonists whose ages range from 18–25, sometimes stretched to 30, and often with college experience. Ultimately, these books feature characters in a post-adolescent phase of life but who have not reached adulthood: 'These novels aim to bring the emotionally intense storylines and fast-paced plotting of young adult fiction to stories that focus on a new range of experiences in life beyond the teenage years' (Wetta 2013). Once again we see the development of a sub-category of literature that responds to the real and perceived needs readers have at specific stages in their life cycle: stages of life that are also historically and culturally contingent. For example, the college experience that so many of these 'emerging adult' novels captures is not a universal experience for many reasons. However, there is clearly enough of a niche for these books to justify a marketing category of their own.

Disciplinary commitments and definitions

Children's Literature as a study draws on the skills of librarians, teachers, literary critics, and others. Each discipline has its own privileged methodologies and concerns. But wherever the institutional home for the study of children's literature is, it is possible, and often desirable, to draw on the theories, methodologies, and texts of multiple disciplines. Literary critics can offer formal understanding of literary language and structure, locate works within the wide sweep of literary history, and historicize the works within their specific literary period. Librarians, literary critics, and teachers all share an interest in questions of censorship, in the effects on the discipline of the major children's literature prizes, and children's access to a wide range of children's literature.

In *Children's Literature Comes of Age* ([1996] 2016), Nikolajeva argues that: 'The notions of childhood and the educational aspects of reading have crucially influenced the evolution of children's literature and have gone hand in hand with pedagogical views of literature as a powerful means for educating children. Children's literature has therefore been studied with a view to the suitability of books for children's reading' (Nikolajeva [1996] 2016, 3). Picking up on the entwined status of children's literature and the field of education, Emer O'Sullivan notes that: 'The general status of children's literature also depends on the relationship between the cultural and educational systems, which can vary greatly within a culture from epoch to epoch' (O'Sullivan 2005a, 19). Karin Lesnik-Oberstein believes that 'it is also still unclear even within the field itself, and despite extensive debates on the issue, what exactly constitutes an "academic" study of children's literature and its criticism as opposed to, say, educational or librarianship courses and publications on children's fiction. In fact, it is disputed whether such a separation is either possible or desirable' (Lesnik-Oberstein 2004, 1).

In the past, some Children's Literature scholars have felt disrespected within English and Literature departments, as Beverly Lyon Clark (2003) notes when she writes about the distortion of the term 'children's literature' to 'kiddie lit.' Clark is particularly interested in the cultural devaluation of children's books from the 19th century to the present, pointing out that many 19th century elites enjoyed and lauded works of children's literature such as *Huckleberry Finn* or *Little Women*. As the prestige of these works slipped they became associated with children, and increasingly derided. She traces this condescension to the historical dominance of women in fields such as education or librarianship. As Clark notes, '[A]ttitudes toward children's literature are never simple; they're always complexly connected to attitudes associated with gender or class or ... a particular profession' (Clark 2003, 75), by which she means the cultural devaluation of librarianship and teaching as feminized vocations. The historical and central role of women in librarianship, teaching, and children's publishing has been explored by Jacalyn Eddy's study of women in children's book publishing from 1919 to 1939 (Eddy 2006) and Anne Lundin's history of the establishment of Children's Literature canons by schools, professional organizations, and libraries (Lundin 2004). Women shaped the world of 19th and early 20th century children's literature and the field of Children's Literature offered them many professional opportunities not otherwise available.

Children's Literature scholarship is increasingly aware of its relationship to other disciplines. For example, Kenneth Kidd's *Freud in Oz: At the Intersections of Psychoanalysis and Children's Literature* (2011) shows that children's literature and psychoanalysis have a mutually constitutive relationship: 'Not only did the serious study of children's literature start with Freud,' Kidd has argued, but we could also say that 'psychoanalysis developed in part through its engagement with children's literature' (Kidd 2011b, vii). At its best, the study of children's literature invites its practitioners to reflect on how and why they approach the subject, how they weigh evidence such as literary responses from children, and what they think the purpose of the experience and study of children's literature is. The field of Children's Literature continues to add to its range of potential methodologies and theoretical possibilities, as Chapter 4 will investigate in greater detail by exploring some recent developments, such as Childhood Studies approaches.

Fully engaged with the nature of disciplinary differences, Karen Coats speaks in practical terms about the limits of any single discipline:

> No one discipline has the last word regarding what defines childhood or what constitutes effective intervention. The best solutions for the problems of individual children are usually going to be situational rather than systemic. Because children in their specificity can be extremely complex, a correspondingly complex array of possibilities and imaginative approaches, informed by a multiplicity of disciplinary strategies, will be most effective for educating the child worker, teacher, researcher, and/ or parent (Coats 2001, 145).

Case study: E.B. White, *Charlotte's Web*

In a recent poll for BBC Culture, E.B. White's *Charlotte's Web* (1952) was named the most popular work for children of all time. One reason, among many, for the book's cultural presence over several decades is its ability to reach out to both child and adult readers. Yet the book is also very clear about the differences between children and adults, not to mention humans and the animal world. It shows a world of talking animals in the barnyard available to children but incomprehensible to adults, sometimes to comic effect as the humans fall for Charlotte's trick and wildly misunderstand the miracle they have witnessed. It is also skilled at capturing the physical and emotional sensations of a protected childhood, with its vulnerable young protagonist Wilbur, who is the runt of a litter of new-born pigs, becoming increasingly cherished. Wilbur receives comfort and protection, first from Fern Avery, a young girl who saves Wilbur from being slaughtered by her father, nursing him tenderly with a bottle, and then by the literate spider Charlotte, who offers him friendship and then, filling something of a maternal role, mounts a successful campaign to convince Wilbur's owner, Mr Zuckerman, not to kill him.

When Wilbur is moved from the Avery home to the Zuckerman barn he is listless and lonely: the loneliness of a child in need of company and nurture, which Charlotte, in becoming his friend, offers him. As he grows, it becomes apparent that his destiny is the slaughterhouse. Charlotte's task then is to convince the farmers that he is an extraordinary pig and should be kept alive. She does this by weaving words into her web: 'SOME PIG,' 'RADIANT,' 'TERRIFIC,' and 'HUMBLE.' In saving Wilbur's life, Charlotte ensures that, in many ways, he never has to grow up: he can remain a protected child forever. At the end of the novel he finds himself in a cyclical world, where life is 'very good—night and day, winter and summer, spring and fall, dull days and bright days. It was the best place to be' (White [1952] 1980, 183). Read this way, the continuity of Wilbur's life inheres in an avoidance of the hard facts of adulthood, an assertion of the pastoral in the face of potential change.

Norton D. Kinghorn, however, sees the novel as embodying 'inevitable, irresistible, implacable change':

> change in two worlds: the world of the barn, of the seasons, all of nature; and the world of humans, who appear in the novel as interlopers, creatures lost to the mysteries of nature, no longer able to fathom the miracle of a spider's web or the chirping of crickets or the coming of spring (Kinghorn 1986, 5).

In some ways this reading depends on an interpretation of the seasons not as a cycle of birth, death, and rebirth, but as indicators of the forward march of time.

Fern's movement away from the world of the barnyard into a fascination with a local boy, Henry Fussy, is one of the text's markers of inevitable change. At the beginning of the novel, Fern can sit for hours in the barn and hear the animals' conversation, albeit as a spectator and not as a participant. Fern's mother, Mrs Avery, is concerned about her daughter and goes to see a medical doctor, Dr Dorian, to ask his advice. Dorian leaves open the possibility that children might see things that adults cannot, but predicts that Fern will probably outgrow the barn in time, which does indeed happen: 'Fern did not come regularly to the barn any more. She was growing up, and was careful to avoid childish things, like sitting on a milk stool near a pigpen' (White [1952] 1980, 183). Even at the fairground, when Wilbur wins a special prize, Fern is off exploring with Henry. John W. Griffith sees Fern as embodying one model of childhood: the feckless child who, like Peter Pan, moves quickly away from attachments and who is hard to pin down (Griffith 1993, 30–31).

Charlotte's Web is also a narrative of someone who faces mortality but is granted a reprieve. It begins with the startling line: 'Where's Papa going with that Ax?' (White [1952] 1980, 1). In this sense it can be read as reflecting the Cold War fears of the time of its publication in 1952, with looming threats that are averted, however temporarily. Yet in its simple but direct account of Charlotte's death, bound together with her sacrifices for Wilbur, the text asks its readers to confront the difficult topic of mortality. In her study of terminally ill children dying of leukaemia, Myra Bluebond-Langner poignantly notes:

> The most popular book among these children was *Charlotte's Web*. When Mary and Jeffrey reached stage 5, it was the only book they would read. Several children at stage 5 asked for chapters of it to be read to them when they were dying. But as one parent stated, 'They never chose the happy chapters.' They always chose the chapter in which Charlotte dies. After any child died, the book had a resurgence of popularity among the others (Bluebond-Langner 1978, 186).

E. B. White's biographer, Scott Elledge, points out how singular and valuable White's novel is when he notes that 'Children's books in the past had seldom faced up so squarely as did *Charlotte's Web* to such truths of the human condition as fear of death, and death itself; and they had not implied the courageous agnosticism that disclaimed any understanding of why life and the world are the way they are' (Elledge 1984, 305). It remains true that Wilbur survives, and Charlotte does not. That has been read in gendered terms as a female sacrifice, perhaps even a maternal sacrifice. We can also see the text as facilitating two sorts of recognition: the need to face the harshest of possible realities, and simultaneously to avoid it.

In some ways *Charlotte's Web* seems like a throwback to the animal fables of classic children's literature. With its talking animals it is clearly an animal fantasy. However, White was quite adamant that the characters were animals and not humans; he had consulted scientists at a natural history museum and he was quite pleased at the 'scholarly accuracy of his text and [Garth] Williams's drawings' (Elledge 1984, 295). White was in this regard the heir of the tradition of Beatrix Potter, where an imaginative and fantastic text was united with a keen-eyed, almost scientific, sense of observation. White believed that 'he helped readers free themselves from prejudices against spiders' (Elledge 1984, 303). Elledge notes: 'In 1952 few children's books have made so clear as *Charlotte's Web* that the natural world of the barn does not exist to serve the world of the farmers who think they own it' (Elledge 1984, 305). At the same time the book sends something of a mixed message about animals, which is not lost on Griffith as he notes that White's 'feeling about animals seems to have been an unusual mixture of the naturalist's love of pure observation, the farmer's businesslike concern for care, feeding, and harvesting, and the pet-lover's pleasure in animals' companionship, enriched by a certain imaginative projection onto them of human personalities' (Griffith 1993, 55). This may be one of the book's signature attributes: its oscillation between different modes of human-animal relationship, even if some of those relationships are read with a critical edge.

Charlotte's Web undeniably displays animals as smarter than people, one source of its humour. People immediately believe Charlotte's woven words. Only one interlocutor suggests that they might not be dealing with an extraordinary pig but with an extraordinary *spider*. In its use of satire, with its knowingness aimed at adult readers, this scene can be seen as 'cross-writing'; it can also be seen as one of the many ways in which the novel initiates novice readers into questions of interpretation.

Charlotte's Web is replete with the contradictions of children's literature. It figures childhood as a protected space away from concerns such as mortality, yet offers the opportunity to face up to death as well. It promises growth and change, yet also works to keep Wilbur's position static and to emphasize a reassuring cyclical world. In this way it embodies the manner in which children's literature reflects a kind of nostalgia for childhood, while elegiacally marking it as all too fleeting.

2

CHILDREN'S LITERATURE: EARLY AND GLOBAL HISTORIES

For a long time the history of children's literature was said to have begun either in the 17th century with the efforts of the Puritans, who considered childhood a particularly urgent time for the saving of souls, or with the commercial publishers of the 18th century, who developed children's literature publishing as a distinct market, largely within an Anglo-American context. However, scholars now 'consider multiple definitions of childhoods and children's literatures' (Lamb 2010, 412), with fresh attention given to childhood reading in pre-modern and early modern periods, more attention to global histories, and more attunement to overlooked regional histories and under-explored literary movements. Recent scholarship has also upended some prevailing narratives about the foundational texts of children's literature. For example, Czech humanist John Amos Comenius is often credited with producing the first picture-book, *Orbis Sensualium Pictus*, published in German in 1658, but Mary Ann Farquhar asserts that China produced such a picture-book a century before: 'an illustrated version of *Daily Stories*, a staple in the Confucian children's canon,' written in 1542 (Farquhar [1999] 2015, 16).

In my first chapter I discussed ways in which the definition of children's literature is strongly rooted in a specific time and place, and how social and cultural institutions shape what we consider 'children's literature.' The study of children's literature reveals much about our conceptions of childhood itself, including sometimes contradictory notions. For example, while the Puritan period stressed religious salvation, several romances and folktales available in the oral and written cultures kept pagan ideals and practices very much in the forefront of childhood reading. While the 19th century ushered in a spirit of anti-didacticism, it also possessed many explicitly didactic works in a variety of genres, including religious tracts, fictions espousing civic virtues, as well as works that underpinned the colonialist project of empire. The history of children's literature at any given moment frequently unfolds as a debate between conflicting ideas of both childhood and its literature. We see this, for example, in the late 18th century tension between a Romantic vision of a child as an avatar of transcendent freedom and an equally strong vision of the child as needing rigorous socialization into social and cultural norms.

It is with an eye to these conflicting ideas about childhood that I have chosen Edward Lear's *A Book of Nonsense* (1846) as my case study for this chapter. In several ways this collection is very much a work of its time: an anti-didactic, playful work of poetry leading into the 'golden age' of children's literature. Yet its strict poetic form affirms the very order it seeks to disrupt. It is a work that embodies some of the contradictions that inhere within the history of children's literature.

Pre-modern children's literature

Recent scholarship asks whether there is something we can term 'children's literature' in earlier periods, predating its ostensible emergence in the 17th or 18th centuries. Gillian Adams has looked at works 'closely associated with children' in the Sumerian civilizations of the Third Dynasty of Ur (from the 22nd to 21st century BC) (Adams 1986, 1). She finds that the Sumerians created **fables** and instructional works stressing values such as hard work, the attainment of status, and material prosperity, but also the cultivation of '"nam-lú-ulù", humanity, a concept which included the practice of truth, goodness, justice, mercy, courage, loyalty, and other virtues' (Adams 1986, 27). These were qualities that made people worthy of the favour of the Gods. Wrestling with whether this pre-print literature was indeed meant for children, Adams described it as 'an imaginative literature which may or may not have been originally composed for younger children or directed at them, but which was considered particularly suitable for them and to which they were regularly exposed' (Adams 1986, 26). It would be impossible to find a more inclusive definition; it stresses children's 'exposure' to literature or their 'association' with it without the obligation to prove that they were imagined as its readers, much less its sole readers.

When trying to find out what children read (or what was read to them) in earlier eras, scholars have often focused on educational conventions and children's attainment of literacy. Sometimes looking at children's books from the past can be a means of exploring literacy and educational practices that are no longer familiar. As Seth Lerer notes of classical antiquity, 'Literary study led to a proficiency in rhetoric, and law, politics, and military leadership that were all rhetorical activities in Greek and Roman culture. To look for children's literature in classical antiquity, therefore, is to look at the history of rhetoric and education' (Lerer 2008, 17). Greek and Roman children were given excerpts from Homer or Virgil with a stress on recitation, memorization, and quotation. Educators of the period sought to break these texts down into 'manageable sections,' with each section **age-levelled** so that 'Different passages would be read at different ages. And, always, texts would be prepared for recitation. Education trained the students to put on new roles: the parent, the teacher, the god, the ruler' (Lerer 2008, 19). Karen Sánchez-Eppler notes, in fact, that the 'preservation of ancient literature depends to a remarkable extent on the plethora of copies of texts produced by Sumero-Babylonian, Egyptian, Greek, and Roman children learning to write' (Sánchez-Eppler 2013, 226).

Michael Levy and Farah Mendlesohn note how children's engagement with literature in classical and ancient times anticipates adulthood, rather than lingering on childhood as a special state:

fiction is a thing *for* children, but not *of* them. It is a route out of childhood and into the adult world which does not treasure the child or childhood as something precious, and in which children's reading is contiguous with that of adults (Levy and Mendlesohn 2016, 11).

Levy and Mendlesohn see this strand of 'civic education' persisting into the 19th century with works like Thomas Hughes' *Tom Brown's Schooldays* (1857). The history of children's literature reflects this ongoing tension between children's books preserving and promoting a 'childlike' quality, and children's books as a way to push children towards adulthood. There has always been a strand of children's literature that does not seek to enable the child 'to be a child' but to move him or her as quickly as possible into a state of maturity.

Scholars have also discerned what we now conceive of as 'childlike' qualities in early modern or pre-modern works. In her studies of medieval texts, Gillian Adams searches for 'as many indications as possible' that something might be considered children's literature (Adams 1998, 11–12). This includes both internal evidence (the address of a child; a child functioning as a character; explanatory glosses directed at 'inexpert readers') and external evidence (appearance in collections meant for schools; references in other works of children's education). Her studies also require sensitivity to the complex registers of the Latin language in which many of these works are written:

> medieval Latin comes in a wide variety of styles and complexities. It has its Dr. Seusses, Virginia Woolfs, and James Joyces, just as other languages do. If a text is short and in very simple Latin, it is proper to ask why this is so. What evidence exists that it is written for semi-literate adults as opposed to children learning how to read? Is there, for example, a more difficult, perhaps more 'adult' version extant? (Adams 1998, 16).

The qualities or markers that distinguish a work as one for children or not for children, as the case may be, continue to preoccupy scholars and theorists in the field: an enduring question even for 20th and 21st century works. Take, for example, the idea that if a main character in a given work is a child, it is probably a work of children's literature. A child protagonist is often a good indicator that a work is aimed at children, but that is not true, for example, of Jonathan Safran Foer's *Extremely Loud & Incredibly Close* (2005), whose quirky nine-year-old protagonist Oskar roams New York City to try to piece together clues about a mysterious key left behind by his father, who was killed in the 9/11 terrorist attacks. In short, the kinds of questions that animate the early history of children's literature remain in force as we contemplate more contemporary texts.

Anyone working on medieval literature must reckon with Philippe Ariès' influential, but now widely challenged, thesis that medieval people did not recognize childhood, as he argued in his *Centuries of Childhood* (first published in 1960 as *L'enfant et la vie familiale sous l'Ancien Régime* and in English in 1962). However, he also noted that this was 'not to suggest that children were neglected, forsaken or despised':

> The idea of childhood is not to be confused with affection for children; it corresponds to an awareness of the particular nature of childhood, that particular nature which distinguishes the child from adult, even the young adult (Ariès 1962: 128).

Historians such as Barbara Hanawalt, Nicholas Orme, and Shulamith Shahar have challenged Ariès and delineated the social institutions and structures that addressed the specific needs and capacities of children, including systems of education. Historians of childhood have elucidated the theories and practices of premodern and early modern life stages, as Adrienne Gavin notes:

> 'Ages of man' divisions of medieval and early modern thought, particularly ages of childhood—*infantia* (up to age 7), *pueritia* (7–14), and *adolescentia* (14 and above)—are also important in the periods' literary constructions of childhood. Being raised in clear stages towards adulthood and/or a Christian afterlife, children in these texts are revealed not simply as 'little adults' but as beings with their own roles, tastes, and thematic resonances (Gavin 2012, 4).

These 'ages of man' should not be confused with modern theories of psychological development, of the kind that we see in the work of Jean Piaget, a 20th century Swiss clinical psychologist who posited that, from birth to age 16, infants and children go through four main developmental stages. Pre-modern and early modern 'ages of man' are perhaps best understood through Gavin's notion of 'roles.' For example, Jaques' speech in Shakespeare's *As You Like It* (1623) compares the world to a play with seven acts or 'seven ages' played by each actor: infant, schoolboy, lover, soldier, justice, pantaloon, and 'second childishness,' which is extreme old age:

> All the world's a stage,
> And all the men and women merely players,
> They have their exits and their entrances;
> And one man in his time plays many parts,
> His acts being seven ages
>
> (Shakespeare, *As You Like It*, Act 2, Scene VII, Lines 138–142).

The pre-modern and early modern 'ages of man' are also calibrated to class. For example, the 'mirror for princes' genre helped prepare future rulers for their elevated roles when they were very young.

Daniel T. Kline acknowledges some of the challenges in his study of medieval literature for children when he suggests that 'the relative paucity of available texts and the difficulties of language make pre-printing press children's literature difficult to study, while the relatively narrow diffusion of manuscript materials makes it difficult to draw any general conclusions about medieval youths' access to literature' (Kline 2003, 2). Peter Hunt muses on our historical distance from children of previous centuries: 'It is difficult to imagine the impact of a chapbook on a child four hundred years ago; was it the equivalent of the impact of a virtual-reality CD hologram on the child of today?' (Hunt 1996, 201). Nonetheless, scholars do make the attempt. As one example among many, Nicholas Orme talks about medieval alphabet books: 'The alphabet, by the twelfth century, was no longer a mere list of letters. It had become Christianized. Saying it was a kind of devotion, beginning with the act of crossing yourself and ending, as all prayers did, with "amen"' (Orme 2006, 56).

Medieval children's literature contains varied genres such as Bible stories, dialogues with 'wise children,' conduct books at least partly directed to youth, and miscellaneous story collections. Chaucer's *A Treatise on the Astrolabe,* about an instrument used to make astronomical measurements, is an example of a book specifically tailored for the instruction of a single child: his son Lewis. Scholars of childhood and children's literature have also gone back to look at dramatic performances such as the morality plays and how they included child audiences and child performers.

Fables like those of Aesop played an important role. Although not translated into dedicated editions for children until the 17th century, they were certainly part of childhood reading. Victoria DeRijke notes, 'Aesop's fables have been adapted for feudal, medieval, clerical, educational use; in fact, the fable form is also part of worldwide acculturation' (DeRijke 2014, 47). For example, the *Panchatantra* (or 'Five Treatises'), an ancient Indian collection written in Sanskrit, has entered the folklore of many countries and been retold many times for children.

Early children's literature emerges from a different socioeconomic and cultural system than ours, including differences in language, generic conventions, and attitudes about childhood. Our sense of the 'literary'—where its boundaries fall— affects our definition of children's literature. When we speak of the medieval treatise or sermon, or the early modern conduct book, we might not think of them as 'literary works.' But the pre-Enlightenment age did not draw strict boundaries between fiction and non-fiction and between the literary and the non-literary. That is one reason why we might explore medieval conduct manuals as works of children's literature.

In our arguably secular age it can also be something of a challenge to acknowledge how the early history of children's literature was shaped by religious aims and conviction, so much so that without this sacred orientation children's literature as a field would not exist. Pat Pinsent notes that 'Much of the material intended for young readers was either directly religious in origin, or took the form of stories calculated to motivate them towards behavior regarded as appropriate to young Christians' (Pinsent 2017, 247). Pinsent, like many, sees continuity as well as change, with the religious feeling of early children's literature transformed into 'the spiritual value of respect for the environment' in contemporary works (Pinsent 2017, 248).

Despite certain continuities, some critics have asserted that contemporary children cannot relate to historical children's books. Since children's literature from earlier periods might embody very different values, or reflect unfamiliar cultural norms, the place of historical children's literature in the reading lives of children today is an open question. In 'Passing on the Past: The Problem of Books That Are for Children and That Were for Children,' Hunt argues that historical children's literature is no longer viable for contemporary children: 'History is marked by fractures, chasms, which readers cannot in the natural way of things cross, and this is particularly true of the history of children's literature and reading' (Hunt 1996, 201). Gillian Adams disagrees, noting that imaginative works from the medieval period appeal to contemporary readers 'when they are well translated' (Adams 1998, 17). She points to the repository of stories in the Western world that draw on medieval themes and narrative structures, including the various iterations of the Reynard the Fox stories and material used by the Grimm brothers. Even if some of this medieval material is adapted or transmuted, it remains a living part of the tradition.

Early children's literature is often felt to be too 'didactic' for modern audiences. The term 'didactic' simply means that a work was meant to teach or instruct. But it can also imply an excessively pedantic manner, or material whose informative function is devoid of any pleasurable elements. However, scholars such as Daniel T. Kline, Gordon Moyles, Patricia Demers, David Rudd, Andrea Immel, Andrew O'Malley, and Mitzi Myers among others have revealed that the didacticism of children's texts before the 19th century was more complex than it originally appeared. Daniel T. Kline argues that there are startling similarities between pre-modern works and more recent writings for children. Contemporary literature 'expresses the social attitudes and anxieties of its era,' just as medieval literature does.

> To take even a cursory survey of children's literature over the last forty years is to read a social history of late-twentieth-century culture. For example, recent award-winning children's books have tackled such contemporary issues as death, divorce, homelessness, disability, natural disaster, racism, violence, and sexuality, addressing those issues with an eye towards facilitating a child's understanding and enriching her experience in a broadly liberal manner (Kline 2003, 3).

In Kline's formulation, the didacticism of the pre-modern period is not worlds away from our own cultural practices. Modern literature teaches young people about the 'social attitudes and anxieties' of our time, just as earlier children's literature did in its time. Klein's remarks help us to acknowledge how much of children's literature aims to teach children the nature and norms of the society into which they will mature.

Klein takes aim here at the idea that didacticism is always disempowering for child readers. Recent researchers have in fact found in didactic works a unique site to explore childhood agency and child power. Merridee L. Bailey stresses 'the direct emphasis on the actions of the child or youth themselves' in medieval **courtesy literature**, an emphasis that reveals 'perceptions of personal autonomy and responsibility at the forefront of the culture of childhood' (Bailey 2007, 30). Although marked by hierarchical organization, and authoritative in its advice, the Anglo-Norman conduct manual *The Babees' Book, or, A Little Report of How Young People Should Behave* (c.1475) assumes that children are able to join the adult world and master its expectations, from table manners to interactions with other people. Early in *The Babees' Book* the author notes:

> I think to show how you babies who dwell in households should 'have yourselves when you be set at meat, and how when men bid you be merry, you should be ready with lovely, sweet and benign words (Rickert, ed. 1908, 2).

While we might hear this authorial voice as a lofty, superior one, it could equally be read as the voice of a kind and wise informant who wants to show young people the ropes, a cultural imperative in the fostering system where young people had to adjust quickly to life outside their family of origin when they were sent to a new household. Juanita Feros Ruys uses the contemporary idea of 'emotional intelligence' to consider 'medieval parental didactic literature':

> they are advising their children about the prevailing emotional *mores* of their social context together with advice as to how they can negotiate these to become successful agents within that context. Indeed, it makes sense that medieval parents would be interested in a form of emotional instruction that encompassed group dynamics in addition to individual affective states, given the importance of group membership in this era (Ruys 2018, 21).

Scholars have also discerned elements in these early texts that militate against their didacticism or offer a subversive subtext in opposition to their explicit messages. David Rudd, for example, looks closely at 'Symon's Lesson of Wisdom for all Manner of Children,' part of *The Babees' Book*, with its admonitions to 'climb not over house nor wall … make no crying, jokes nor plays/ In holy Church on holy days.' He concludes: 'While authority can be seen wagging its finger, the author simultaneously provides a list of pranks for the child's delectation' (Rudd 2013, 32). Seeing the pleasures in didactic literature sometimes involves reading against the grain, as Rudd does here.

Readers in the pre-modern and early modern periods did not feel compelled to make a choice between 'instruction' and 'delight,' feeling instead that the didactic and the pleasurable could be co-mingled, and certainly that both might have a role to play in childhood reading. For example, John Comenius's *Orbis Sensualium Pictus,* an early non-fiction picture-book, declares the intention to teach children 'by sport and merry pastime' (Comenius 1659, A4v). Illustrations form part of this pleasurable teaching: 'Children (even from their Infancy almost) are delighted with Pictures, and willingly please their eyes with these sights'

(Comenius 1659, A4r). This is not to assume that all children's texts, early or contemporary, balance pleasure and instruction. It does, however, challenge scholarly accounts that paint an image of earlier children's literature as marked only by a grim didacticism. Later in this chapter we will consider how recent scholars have looked more sympathetically at the '**rational moralists,**' a group of writers in the 18th century who stressed the power of didactic children's literature to cultivate young people's reason.

Moving towards a dedicated literature for children

Technological innovation was a major contributing factor to the development of children's books, with the advent of the printing press and technologies such as the **hornbook**. The hornbook was originally a primer for study, where a sheet of paper with the letters of the alphabet or a religious text was mounted on a wooden frame with a protective sheet of transparent horn (or bone). Hornbooks, used from the 15th to 18th centuries, often had a hole punched in the handle so they could hang from a child's belt or girdle. **Battledores** were a related technology, with a similar shape but made from cardboard with a paper overlay; they dropped out of production in the 19th century. **Chapbooks** were also popular; these were inexpensive booklets written in a wide variety of genres including tales of adventure, folk, and fairy tales. Chapbooks were read by children and adults alike and are often regarded as one of the first iterations of 'popular culture.'

Renaissance humanism also had an impact on children's literature, since it fuelled secular, as opposed to sacred, learning and encouraged a return to Greek and Roman thought. Roger Ascham's *The Schoolmaster* (1570) is one example of such a book. Not intended for schools, *The Schoolmaster* focused on the teaching of Latin for individual youths in the houses of gentlemen and noblemen. In some ways, the early modern period can be seen as a reinvigoration of some of the ancient and classical traditions discussed by Lerer in his history of children's literature. In other ways, the development of new technologies anticipated the development of children's literature as a separate phenomenon for children. Edel Lamb notes, 'the expansion of print culture in England during the sixteenth and seventeenth centuries resulted in a significant increase in the range of texts produced for children' (Lamb 2012, 70).

Many scholars contend that the 17th century was the time when a distinct children's literature began to emerge. Maria Nikolajeva's remarks are typical of this approach: 'The very emergence of children's literature on a large scale is due to the fact that sometime in the seventeenth century society became conscious of childhood as a special period of life and that children had their own special needs' (Nikolajeva [1996] 2016, 3). One group frequently credited with a distinct children's literature is comprised of the English **Puritans**, an amorphous religious group that refused to conform to the requirements of the national religion as practised by the Church of England, feeling that its organization and forms of worship needed both reform and simplification. To Puritans, the Church of England still included too many Catholic elements in its organization and worship practice, making the Protestant reformation incomplete.

In Seth Lerer's words, 'Puritanism was a movement for the future,' insofar as it sought quite radical change (Lerer 2008, 81). This future orientation involved commitment to the kind of literacy that became newly urgent after the Protestant reformation, as individuals were granted the opportunity—and given the responsibility—to engage with scripture on their own. In the late 17th century and after the restoration of the monarchy, John Bunyan's *The Pilgrim's Progress* (1678) was one of the most important Puritan texts, subsequently widely adapted for children. This allegorical story of Christian's journey through spaces such as the Slough of Despond and Vanity Fair, and his struggles with Apollyon the monster, offered not only a vivid and concrete representation of abstract spiritual values but also vicarious participation in the protagonist's journey. As late as Louisa May Alcott's *Little Women* (1868–1869), the young girls in the novel are still using Bunyan's formulation to guide their play. Alcott structures her novel in accordance with its various incidents and scenes.

The Puritans are also known for the 'joyful death' tradition, most notably James Janeway's *A Token for Children* (1671). In a preface directed to parents, Janeway severely asks: 'Are the Souls of your Children of no value? … They are not too little to dye, they are not too little to go to Hell, they are not too little to serve their great Master, too little to go to Heaven, *For of such is the Kingdom of God'* (Janeway [1671] 1676, A3v–A4r). Several of Janeway's own brothers had died of tuberculosis; he lived in London during the great plague, and so the pious words and deaths of children felt urgent to him personally. Cotton Mather, a New England preacher, wrote his own version, *A Token, for the Children of New England* (1700), and attached his version to Janeway's in the New England edition.

To contemporary readers, the 'joyful deaths' tradition might seem alien due to both its resolute piety and its unflinching engagement with the deaths of very young children. Yet *A Token for Children* must have appealed to some portion of the reading public to be so frequently reprinted; perhaps the courage of the children and their heightened spiritual awareness impressed young readers. Perhaps they appreciated a book that engaged with their worst fears and helped them face up to them. We might think of a contemporary work such as John Green's *The Fault in Our Stars* (2012) as a throwback to this older tradition, with the philosophical discoveries made by teenage characters like Hazel Grace Lancaster and Augustus Waters as they face their terminal illnesses (Coats 2018, 21).

Puritan children's writers did reach out deliberately to child readers. Bunyan's poetry book, *A Book for Boys and Girls, or Country Rhimes for Children* (1686), for example, appeals to children's sensibilities in 74 short verses meant to capture spiritual realities; in one, 'Upon the Frog,' religious hypocrites are compared to the slippery titular amphibian. Isaac Watts wrote gentle lyrics for children espousing piety and morality, publishing *Divine Songs Attempted in Easy Language for the Use of Children* in 1715. Watts' poems became part of the hymn tradition, with such well-known works as 'Joy to the World' and 'O God, our help in ages past.' Roderick Cave and Sara Ayad note: 'In these poems written for children it is clear he recognized that gentleness in tone was far more likely to engage juvenile minds than making them afraid' (Cave and Ayad 2017, 73).

When considering the social and political thought that shaped the development of children's literature in the Anglo-American world specifically, John Locke's *Some Thoughts Concerning Education* (1693) is a landmark text in many ways. For Locke, children are a *tabula rasa*—or blank slate—needing sensory experience to gain human knowledge. Locke argued, first of all, that innate ideas did not exist, which implied that individuals were the products of their education; as Lerer observes, 'by focusing that education on sensible experience, writers of children's literature could tell stories of growth as encounters with the things of this world' (Lerer 2008, 105). Locke also urged parents to make children's literature as pleasurable as possible, while cultivating reason and virtue.

With this stress on the 'things of this world,' it is hardly surprising that one of the subsequent developments of children's literature in the 18th century is the growth of a commercialized children's literature, emerging, in the words of Andrew O'Malley, as a 'complex nexus of historical, economic, social and cultural factors unique to this period in England' (O'Malley 2004, 1). For O'Malley and other critics, the 18th century is the moment when 'child' audiences were separated from 'adult' audiences (O'Malley 2004).

This period saw the emergence of booksellers who worked with authors to produce commercially viable books. Mary Cooper's *Tommy Thumb's Pretty Song Book for All Little Masters and Misses* (1744) was the earliest collection of nursery rhymes, with 39 rhymes including 'Bah, Bah, a black sheep' and 'Lady Bird, Lady Bird.' Another innovator was Thomas Boreman, whose *Gigantick Histories of the Two Famous Giants and other Curiosities in Guildhall, London* appeared in 1740. Cave and Ayad comment:

> He must have realized that small books would attract children and (in combination with printers, illustrators and bookbinders), he developed a very small format, with the books' pages measuring around 6 x 5 cm. These very small books dealt with very large subjects—giants and monuments—and the books' miniature charms were increased by their attractive bindings (Cave and Ayad 2017, 108).

Histories of children's literature often name John Newbery's *A Little Pretty Pocketbook* (1744) as the first book of children's literature. Newbery is said to have created 'the first children's book' because he also includes toys marketed to children (a pincushion for girls and a ball for boys). Noel Chevalier and Min Wild note perceptively, 'Newbery recognized the importance of being what we today would call a "brand"' (Chevalier and Wild 2013, 126). Books emerge as consumer products that can be made specifically for children, and sold *to* them, or that can be bought for children as an act of love, care, or instruction. This involves, as we have seen, a consideration of the design and format of books for children. For example, William McCarthy credits Anna Laetitia Barbauld with 'the use of large type and wide margins to make the books reader friendly' in *Lessons for Children* (McCarthy 2005, 88). In this period, and moving into the 19th century, there were clear economic motivations to write and publish children's literature. Speaking of the publication of 18th century nursery rhymes, Cave and Ayad note: 'The reasons were commercial and technological: there was a need for awareness that such productions could be profitable, that they could be distributed widely through the country (and in the colonies), and that they would be attractive to potential buyers and the children for whom the books would be purchased' (Cave and Ayad, 2017, 16). M.O. Grenby notes that this emerging trade depended not just on producers and distributors, but also on the zeal and commitment of book users of various kinds: 'it was the first consumers whose willingness to purchase, at extra expense, a separate set of books for children enabled the form to live and later thrive' (Grenby 2011, 289). He notes the presence of many gift books, which in his estimation challenges 'any assumption that early children's books were bought primarily as instruments of education and improvement' (Grenby 2011, 285).

Mary V. Jackson argues that children's literature helped contribute to the expansion of the middle classes 'for they helped to promulgate ideals of polite social usage as surely as they sharpened worldly ambition. Thus, just as we can chart a shift in the literature from otherworldly *piety* to pious social *propriety*, so also can we trace the diffusion of ideals of social refinement'

(Jackson 1989, 55–56). One of the landmark texts of the period, often described as the first novel for children, is Sarah Fielding's *The Governess* (1749). Set in an all-girl's school, *The Governess* weaves the life stories of the pupils with moral advice from their governess, Mrs Teachum, interspersed with fairy tales. Fielding's book is a clear addition to the literature of social refinement outlined by Jackson.

Many of the producers of children's literature imagined it as the articulation of a new 'middle-class' identity designed to purge children's literature of its plebian roots, although these works also contained less refined elements. For example, Newbery's *A Little Pretty Pocket Book* (1744) included the story of 'Jack the Giant Killer,' a character from the older, plebian tradition of the chapbooks. Once again an evolutionary history which offers a story of children's literature as constantly improving, and getting closer to the needs of children, requires to be supplanted by one that acknowledges both continuity and change.

Given the emerging market forces that shaped children's literature, should the definition of children's literature be predicated on its growth as a commercial form? Gillian Adams, for example, objects to the idea that the 'very existence' of children's literature 'as a separate entity is tied to commercial interests' (Adams 1998, 19). Research on children's literature before the 18th century challenges the notion that children's literature needs its own economic niche to exist, as we see in Adams' own work on ancient Sumer or on medieval literature. It is hard to deny that consumer forces from the 18th century onward have indelibly shaped children's literature. Whether the very definition of children's literature should be staked on those consumer interests is another matter.

What the child should signify: Evangelicals, Romantics, and rational moralists

Continuing with the notion that children's literature possesses contradictions in each part of its history, David Rudd, engaging with Andrew O'Malley's work, notes that childhood in the late 18th century 'saw a huge struggle over what the child should signify' (Rudd 2013, 24). Elaine Ostry notes three main discourses that share 'a concern with the roles of morality and fancy in children's literature' (Ostry 2002, 36). These are the **Evangelicals**, with their focus on religious salvation, the **rational moralists**, who stressed the inculcation of reason in young people, and the **Romantics**, who sought imaginative freedom for their children. Ostry notes the difficulty in classifying many of the tales children read in the 19th century: 'the author may be known as an Evangelical, but writes a fairy tale, a form disparaged by strict Evangelicals as a lie. Or a fanciful tale has a strong tone of moral didacticism, which is what the fantasists claimed to avoid' (Ostry 2002, 36–37). With this caution in mind, it is nonetheless helpful to consider how late 18th and early 19th century children's literature is marked by competing ideals of children's reading.

As we noted earlier, much of the history of children's literature in the Anglo-American world is bound up with religious practice, and the Evangelical movement of the 18th and early 19th centuries is no exception. Anna Laetitia Barbauld published *Hymns in Prose for Children* (1781), and Hannah More, a founder of the Sunday School movement, produced the Cheap Repository Tracts, which contained moral tales.

The rational moralists were a group of authors and educators that included Mary Wollstonecraft and Maria Edgeworth, working with her father Richard Edgeworth. They believed that children's literature had a particular responsibility to cultivate the child's independent reasoning. We see this unfold in one famous story, Edgeworth's 'The Purple Jar,' in which seven-year-old Rosamond is tempted in a London shop by a beguiling purple jar filled with liquid. She begs her mother to buy it, but is cautioned that there is not enough money to buy both the new shoes she urgently needs and the pretty jar. Rosamond persists, but the jar turns out to be an ordinary clear glass jar filled with a foul-smelling liquid. Rosamond's shoes become increasingly worn, to the point that she can no longer walk in them, and her disgusted father excludes her from a family outing rather than allow her out with such inadequate footwear. Many have found the mother in the story unsympathetic, and Rosamond's attraction to sensual beauty has struck a chord with many appreciative readers. Yet such works, in the words of Adrienne Gavin, 'emphasize the need for children to make rational decisions and bear the consequences of giving in to irrational desires' (Gavin 2012, 8). Feminist scholars have also drawn attention to the 'rational mother-teachers like Rosamond's, the educating heroines of girls' fiction who helped keep alive enlightened notions of female education in the reactionary period of the French wars' (Myers 1989, 54). The rationalist moralists were determined to educate girls as well as boys, 'granting girlhood the potentiality for rational agency and self-command' (Myers 1989, 55).

The rational moralists were often dismissed as humourless and heavy-handed, but Mitzi Myers was one of the first critics to open up an understanding of their aesthetic and cultural virtues, as we see in her astute remarks about Richard and Maria Edgeworth's *Practical Education* (1798):

> The 'practical' in *Practical Education*'s title ... means, not 'utilitarian' as it is sometimes misread, but grounded in real life, everyday experience of child minds and child nature, rather than in theory, and the book is chockful of lively anecdotes of actual children's doings and sayings to illustrate points (Myers 1989, 54).

This inclusion of children's actual voices in some ways connects to contemporary engagements with children as readers, which are self-consciously attentive to children's 'doings and sayings.'

Because they are literary works, tales by Edgeworth and others are, to be sure, multivalent. Within many a tale of discipline and self-control, as we have already seen, lies a streak of mischief. David Rudd cites several of Edgeworth's contemporaries who expressed pleasure that, like Rosamond, they struggle to attain self-control, often retaining a streak of the naughty and untameable that becomes associated with such children's literature protagonists as Dennis the Menace, Pippi Longstocking, or the early Anne of Green Gables (Rudd 2013, 91). Mary V. Jackson notes perceptively: 'What saves these stories is the little girl who, unlike her meek, dutiful, dull sister ... is innocently incorrigible. She *intends* to do right, means to recall the rules, but all too humanly forgets' (Jackson 1989, 163).

Roderick McGillis points out that the early history of children's literature is animated by a tension between our desires to let children indulge their own instincts as freely as possible and an equally pressing sense that they are in need of guidance:

> children's literature and culture are the products of a schizoid beginning: they manifest a society's desire to protect and nurture the young for social reasons and a contrasting desire to preserve the individuality of the child as the site of that which we—adults—desire (McGillis 2002, 7).

It is fascinating to see such a contradiction at work in tales such as 'The Purple Jar,' where the reader both sympathizes with Rosamond's headstrong desire for the prettiest and flashiest thing, as an affirmation of her own desires and pleasures, and the knowledge that she must learn to curb those desires to avoid disappointment.

From a contemporary viewpoint, the rational moralists seem prescient about some of the woes and temptations of a consumerist society. In a later 'Rosamond' story, 'The Bracelet of Memory,' Rosamond encounters a travelling salesman who presents her with a variety of mechanical wonders, among them a bracelet that pricks its wearer when 'there is anything you wish to remember at a particular hour, or minute, this day ... the prick of this talismanic bracelet shall remind you of it, true to the second' (Edgeworth [1821] 1836, 275). Invented in Geneva, it anticipates the 'smart watches' of today. Rosamond's father offers her a choice between a very useful horse and this appealing 'bauble.' With her newfound maturity she decides to forgo the watch in favour of the more practical horse, with her family's approval. While Rosamond makes mistakes throughout the various story sequences devoted to her, she is able to resist buying what we today would call 'the latest thing.' Early children's literature can sometimes anticipate some of our ongoing cultural dilemmas.

Romanticism had an enormous impact on the literature and culture of childhood, creating a fresh vision of the romantic child, summarized by Rudd as: 'one with nature, beginning as a blank slate outside the complexities of language, hence requiring vocabulary that is simple and transparent' (Rudd 2013, 24). Like any transnational aesthetic movement, Romanticism is complex, but it could be described as stressing subjective experience, supernatural or non-rational experiences, and sensitivity to the natural world. One key difference between the Romantics and the rational moralists, in the words of James Holt McGavran, Jr. and Jennifer Smith Daniel, is that 'children had special knowledge to teach their elders as well as the other way around' (McGavran and Smith Daniel 2012, xiii).

Jean-Jacques Rousseau's *Émile, or On Education* (1763, first published in French as *Émile, ou De l'éducation*, 1762) was particularly influential. Rousseau was convinced that children were innately good and that they should develop their own potential freely and without interference. Émile is a child raised in isolation and educated by a tutor who answers only his spontaneous questions; Rousseau's book is about both education and humankind in its natural state. Yet we see another contradiction here: this theory of the free development of the child involves locking her/him up in a state of isolation.

The one book allowed to Émile is Daniel Defoe's *Robinson Crusoe* (1719), described by Rousseau as 'the most felicitous treatise on natural education.' In the words of Andrew O'Malley, *Crusoe*

> was not born a children's story but was made one by virtue of its sometimes surprising articulation with ideas that were crystallizing around children in the period: how they should be educated, what their relation to their parents should be, and how they were coming to embody, symbolically, both the promise of the future and a longing for the innocence of the past (O'Malley 2012, 87).

For Rousseau and the Romantic philosophers he influenced, Crusoe's engagement with the material world of the island was the best possible education, entirely unmediated by social relations and the complications of human culture. Rousseau only advised reading half of the book: the material about shipwreck and survival. Of course, in its unabridged form, adult readers can see in *Crusoe* an abundance of disturbing social relationships, in Crusoe's ownership of plantations and Crusoe the master's subjugation of Friday as a slave. But the solitary man on an island was, in the Romantic period, meant to embody a certain form of experience particularly salutary for children.

Romanticism also lauded the ecstasy and spiritual insight of children. Anne Lundin notes that Wordsworth, Coleridge, Blake, Byron, Shelley, and Keats were 'a group associated with a philosophical stance on creativity, perception, and cognition and with popular tropes of pastoral bliss and childhood reverie' (Lundin 2004, 5). Lundin's own work deals with the impact of Romanticism on American librarianship in the 19th and 20th centuries: '[t]he language of children's librarians resembles a Romantic text, full of childhood reverie, paeans to the power of imagination, commitment to a revolutionary cause, and a legitimization of a canon and character to literary selection and guidance' (Lundin 2004, 6).

Ongoing research has complicated our vision of Romanticism. McGavran and Smith Daniel argue that, even at its peak, the lived reality of childhood and the Romantic ideal were not in alignment with each other:

> Some recent scholars seem to want, from a variety of critical stances—Marxist, poststructuralist, psychoanalytic—to dismantle the Romantic concept that childhood is a special time, lamenting that childhood is dead or in crisis or positioning the Child as an Other sealed away both in time and within the brain of the adult. Few of them recognize how deeply the sense of crisis—of repeated threats to children and childhood across time, class, race, and gender—is embedded in the Romantic concept itself; to phrase it alternatively, carefree childhood is a myth, and not one promulgated by Wordsworth, at least not intentionally. As [Steven] Mintz has stated it, "We cling to a fantasy that once upon a time childhood and youth were years of carefree adventure, despite the fact that for most young people in the past, growing up was anything but easy" (McGavran and Smith Daniel 2012, xv).

Historically (as now) a carefree childhood functions more as myth than reality, and some of the writers credited with it may require to be read anew for signs of the strains and fissures in their depiction of innocence and pleasure. Nonetheless, the Romantic ideal of childhood persists not only in the popular imagination but also within the assumptions of many scholars and children's advocates.

Anti-didacticism and the 'golden age' of children's literature

The 'golden age' is termed as such in part because many of the books acknowledged as classics today were published then, from 1865–1915. Lewis Carroll's 1865 *Alice's Adventures in Wonderland* is often cited as the major turning point. This is due largely to its affirmation of the nonsensical over the educational and by its razor-sharp parodies of childhood lessons and didactic verses, such as those by Isaac Watts, whose 'How doth the little busy bee' is transformed into the amoral and nonsensical 'How doth the little crocodile.' For many critics, the 19th century 'golden age' of children's literature is when children's literature *as we know it now* begins, as we see in F.J. Harvey Darton's classic formulation: 'it was the coming to the surface, powerfully and permanently, the first un-apologetic appearance in print, for readers who sorely needed it, of liberty of thought in children's books' (Darton [1932] 1982, 260). The 'golden age' had its fantasists, such as George MacDonald, who created religiously inspired fantasy tales; its books that sought to inspire sympathy for animals (Anna Sewell's *Black Beauty*, 1877); and its domestic morality stories, such as Frances Hodgson Burnett's *A Little Princess* (1905), the story of a virtuous orphan who is restored to the prosperity that is hers by right. We find in the 19th century books that prepared young boys for leadership in an age of empire, among them Thomas Hughes's *Tom Brown's Schooldays* (1857). There is a marked gender split in terms of genre, with books of adventure and exploration marketed more and more towards boys, and domestic fiction marketed to girls. The 'golden age,' much praised as a zenith of children's imaginative culture, registered the contradictions and complications of any other period of the literary history of children's literature: engaging with the Romantic vision of childhood while registering some of the Victorian period's cultural, economic, and political shifts such as industrialism, class struggle, and urbanization. The character of Sissy Jupe in Charles Dickens' *Hard Times* (1854) offers an intriguing example of the Victorian tension between imagination and mechanistic, rational ways of thinking. Her teacher, Mr Gradgrind, asks Sissy, who is the daughter of a circus performer who breaks horses, to define a horse. Addressing her as 'girl number twenty,' he notes that he is looking only for facts. She is unable to produce such a purely factual definition, unlike her classmate Bitzer, who offers:

> Quadruped. Graminivorous. Forty teeth, namely twenty-four grinders, four eye-teeth, and twelve incisive. Sheds coat in the spring; in marshy countries, sheds hoofs too. Hoofs hard but requiring to be shod with iron. Age known by marks in mouth (Dickens 1854, 7).

This definition is the quintessence of the mechanistic and soulless rationality that Gradgrind was looking for. In contrast, Sissy represents creativity and wonderment, gained from her life in the circus. Intriguingly she is also the most practical and sensible of all the characters in the novel, and she helps them change their way of life when it is clearly unsuitable for them. Sissy finds the harmony between imagination and rationality that so many of the other characters lack.

Anne Lundin points out that 'Many of the best-selling novels of the nineteenth century were works we now consider children's literature,' written for a dual audience (Lundin 2004: 60). Beverly Lyon Clark (2003) argues that, in the 19th century, books like Burnett's *Little Lord Fauntleroy* (1885) were appreciated by adults and children alike. Echoing Harry Steele Commager, Clark notes that '[t]he nineteenth century was a time "when majors wrote for minors."' (Clark 2003, 48). But these audiences increasingly split from each other in the early 20th century, with the result that many of these works for children were subsequently devalued in terms of the mainstream literary canon. At the same time, several of these works were reinvented as 'classics' and marked by the determination of older generations to pass on this material to younger generations.

Modernism and the avant-garde

In *The Case of Peter Pan* (1984), Jacqueline Rose argued that children's literature was firmly cut off from **modernism** and from '**avant-garde**' movements, including experimental art forms such as surrealism, Dadaism, and pop-art. However, critical re-evaluation has revealed that children's literature had a profound role to play in modernism and was in its turn influenced by modernist and avant-garde movements. Juliet Dusinberre's *Alice to the Lighthouse: Children's Books and Radical Experiments in Art* ([1987] 1999) showed how so-called high modernist authors like James Joyce and Virginia Woolf were deeply influenced by the formal and cultural innovations of the 'golden age' of children's literature: 'Radical experiments in the arts in the early modern period began in the books which Lewis Carroll and his successors wrote for children' (Dusinberre [1987] 1999, 5). Here, by the phrase 'early modern,' Dusinberre means the modernist movements of the early 20th century, and the kinds of radical experiments covered include everything from stream of consciousness to nonsensical language play and rapid shifts of perspective, all of which are present in some way in Carroll's *Alice* books. Kimberley Reynolds, in her work on radical children's literature, identified experimental and radical forms of children's literature as harbingers of other forms of social change. If daring innovation is possible in children's literature, what kinds of transformation can be effected in the sphere of the political and social?

Modernist and avant-garde children's literature has also been considered within the frame of transnational aesthetic movements, as we see in Bettina Kümmerling-Meibauer and Elina Druker's edited collection, *Children's Literature and the Avant-Garde* (2016), which demonstrates how children's literature was influenced by movements such as pop-art, experimental film, the global impact of geometric design in Soviet picture-books, and many other avant-garde forms and conventions: 'What is manifested in these children's books is a general idea of progression and change—change in norms and mindsets, and changes that can be traced to movements within arts, education, social systems, and ideologies' (Druker and Kümmerling-Meibauer 2015, 8).

There has also been renewed interest in children's literature in terms of modern and postmodern engagement with technology. For Nathalie op de Beeck, 'children's texts of the twenties and thirties pursued a national myth of progress in a proletarian vein, fetishizing powerful machinery and human labor alike' (op de Beeck 2010, 119). According to op de Beeck, 'American picture books and illustrated texts respond to cultural uncertainty with the fairy tale of modernity ... they tend to demystify mass production to show humans and machines working as intimate partners, or to introduce uncanny machines operating solo but doing beneficial deeds' (op de Beeck 2010, 140). The Romantic era privileged what James Kincaid terms 'the Child Botanical,' but the 20th and 21st centuries saw the rise of what Patrick Cox names the 'Child Mechanical':

> The Child Mechanical is a representation of childhood associated with machinery, an image built in American and Western European children's literature, media, and toys that connects the fragility of childhood to the strength and capacity for power and destruction characteristic of large machinery (Cox 2016, 20).

Some of the association of childhood with machinery and technology hearkens to a notion of children as 'early adopters' of technological and social innovation. Others point to the kinds of posthumanism that I will explore more in Chapter 5. We see in the association of children's literature and the mechanical a changing sense of childhood away from the pastoral and towards the technological, but also a sense of children's literature serving the emerging economic and social needs of industrialization.

Children's literature as challenge to periodization

Some critical conceptions of children's literature move it entirely away from literary periods, arguing that children's literature is one of the best literary fields from which to challenge prevailing notions of literary history. Karin E. Westman, in 'Beyond Periodization: Children's Literature, Genre, and Remediating Literary History,' contends that Children's Literature scholars tend to organize the field around genre rather than chronology, locating genres such as 'verse,' 'picture books,' 'science fiction' or 'adventure fiction' across periods. For Westman, children's literature provides a fresh 'organizing principle for literary history' (Westman 2013, 464):

> Thanks to genre's negotiation between convention and innovation, between form and audience, between style and historical specificity, children's literature writes large the ability of genre to ground a text in the initial moments of historical production, the moments of re-production, and the moments of reception. Through generic remediation, children's literature—more than other literatures—eludes conventions of periodization. As a result, by attending to genre, the very category which has relegated children's literature beyond the canonical pale, scholars of children's literature can revise existing narratives of literary history (Westman 2013, 466).

One reason that children's literature can elude conventions of periodization, argues Westman, is that 'It can be difficult to *find* children's literature within the broader landscape of literary history' (Westman 2013, 466). Scholars, therefore, tend to emphasize genre more. In particular, Westman points to genre as **performative**, by which she means it shifts with each context and between generations. Westman's case study for this assertion is Margaret Wise Brown and Clement Hurd's 1947 *Goodnight Moon*, a text that has not been 'claimed' by modernist scholars but one that has over several decades been established as a children's classic. The text of *Goodnight Moon* is spare and lyrical, bringing to mind modernist writers such as Gertrude Stein and the imagist H.D. The bright and simple visuals created by Hurd are reminiscent of modernist painters like Picasso and Matisse. But Westman asks: 'To which "period" does *Goodnight Moon* belong, if it exists in many? The answer does not lie with the ahistorical or the synchronic, but resides instead with multiple and varied instances of generic performance across established periods' (Westman 2013, 467). *Goodnight Moon*, then, belongs to children's literature, not to modernism. Such performance of genres across time periods can be very helpful in encouraging us to attend to the ways in which the same text transforms and morphs through time for different audiences, belonging less to one period than to multiple periods. Generic performance takes precedence over the temporal pressures of historical change.

In her earlier reflections on children's literature and modernism, Westman considers other ways in which children's texts are removed or deracinated from their historical roots:

> For many readers, the best children's books transcend the limits of a single generation to speak to future generations. While literature in general often aspires to this goal, children's literature seems particularly susceptible to losing its historical grounding. In other words, for many readers, good 'adult' literature can be both historical and ahistorical; good children's literature is frequently ahistorical, unless proven otherwise. As a result, genre becomes the way to categorize its texts (Westman 2007, 284).

One way in which Westman's remarks are borne out is in the many excellent histories of genre. As one example of many, Michael Levy and Farah Mendlesohn's *Children's Fantasy Literature: An Introduction* (Levy and Mendlesohn 2016) roots the genre in the fantastic tales of the 16th century but moves forward through figures such as Lewis Carroll, L. Frank Baum, C.S. Lewis, Roald Dahl, and J.K. Rowling, with attention to the ways these authors have shaped the popular imagination. The fairy tale is another genre that could be seen as unbound by chronological periods. The fairy tale is, of course, a major genre within children's literature, even though fairy tales were not originally meant for children. Fairy tales by Charles Perrault, Madame D'Aulnoy, the Brothers Grimm, Hans Christian Andersen, and Oscar Wilde are central to children's literature. They have both an oral and a written history that crosses multiple centuries, even extending back to ancient mythological roots. In some ways the fairy tale is the perfect genre to think about trans-temporality, since it seems to exude a self-conscious 'timelessness.' Fairy tales have their own organization as a genre quite apart from periodization.

Westman's ideas about how children's literature seems to escape historical placement do, then, ring true in many ways. She pinpoints a cultural desire to think of children's literature as 'timeless,' yet it is also true that much invigorating work in the field seeks to restore children's literature to its historical and cultural contexts. Going back to the example of Margaret Wise Brown, for example, Leonard Marcus has tied Brown back to the aesthetic concerns of the modernist movement, also noting that she edited arch-modernist Gertrude Stein's book for children: *The World is Round* (1939). Therefore, even though Westman argues that we do not tend to think of *Goodnight Moon* within the modernist context, some scholars attempt to do so. Thus, an understanding of children's literature as ahistorical quickly gives way to an understanding of children's books as embedded in their literary periods in complex ways.

Global histories

Critics now grapple with the need to consider a more global history that moves beyond the Anglo-American framework. Such an expansive focus is challenging for several reasons: it involves breaking through language and culture barriers, understanding more than one national or regional history, and challenging disciplinary boundaries to work across fields.

Karen Sands-O'Connor describes 'internationalism' as 'increasingly focused on global movement, multiple voices, and the clash of ideologies between groups that might or might not be tied to a particular nationality.' She explains:

> Children's publishing has also changed, becoming at once more global and more local. International organizations such as the International Board on Books for Youth (IBBY) were organized after World War II, and slowly began to recognize authors and illustrators outside of Europe and North America (IBBY's Hans Christian Andersen Award, established in 1956, recognized its first non-European, non-American author, Brazilian Lygia Bojunga Nunes, in 1982). Efforts to promote local children's publishing on an international stage have also been helped by technology through websites like the International Children's Digital Library, established in 2002 (Sands-O'Connor 2014, 3).

Scholars have responded in various ways to the call to internationalize the field. There is an International Research Society for Children's Literature, with participation from more than 40 countries and an explicit goal of creating communication between scholars across the world. The Children's Literature Association, based in North America, notes on its website that it 'actively pursues the internationalization of North American children's literature research by broadening the spectrum of primary and secondary literature discussed at the annual meetings and in the publications of ChLA.' Klaus Doderer's 1975–1982 *Lexikon der Kinder- und Jugendliteratur* and Peter Hunt's *International Companion Encyclopedia of Children's Literature* (Second Edition, 2004) are two examples of children's literature reference sources with an international focus.

Some of the impulse towards a more global children's literature emerged from the crucibles of the two world wars, with a sentimental vision of a 'universal republic of childhood' out of which a brighter future would be built. However, Emer O'Sullivan, for example, expresses scepticism towards this cultural project. She characterizes a work like Paul Hazard's *Les Livres, les enfants et les Hommes* (1932), published after the First World War, as 'a site on which adult difficulties are addressed and often placated; it is about promises which the adults' generations could not keep, amongst them international understanding and world peace' (O'Sullivan 2005a, 9).

Yet O'Sullivan does see some promise in the notion of a 'universal republic of childhood':

> criticism of the enthusiastic over-estimation of the potential beneficial effects of children's literature should not make us forget that post-war measures to foster literary exchange in the cause of international understanding did encourage a generally open-minded attitude towards the literature of other nations. This is particularly clear from the work of the International Youth Library (IYL) and its founder Jella Lepman. In 1946 Lepman turned to twenty nations, most of which had been at war with Germany only a year before, asking for donations to set up an exhibit of children's literature in Munich (O'Sullivan, 2005a, 9).

O'Sullivan has called eloquently for a comparative children's literature focused on cross-cultural transmissions of individual works for children, considering what is lost and gained in translation. One of the biggest impediments to a genuinely global approach to children's literature is that 'The children's book industry in the United States, the leading market, is increasingly dominated by a handful of large media conglomerates whose publishing operations are small sections of their entertainment businesses' (O'Sullivan 2005b: 189). Furthermore, these large media conglomerates have a global reach, as 'they sell their products beyond the borders of individual countries, further changing and globalizing what were once regionally contained children's cultures' (O'Sullivan 2005b, 189). Comparative children's literature, then, is 'a natural site in which to tease out the implications of these recent developments' as 'a discipline that engages with phenomena that transcend cultural and linguistic borders and also with specific social, literary, and linguistic contexts' (O'Sullivan 2005b, 189). Like many emerging methodologies in the field of Children's Literature, O'Sullivan's work puts two academic fields into conversation with each other, noting that Children's Literature has much to contribute to the discipline of Comparative Literature, opening up a new *corpus* of literary works for consideration. In its turn, Children's Literature can benefit from a comparatist approach; this includes the study of genre, comparative histories, the theorization of children's literature itself, comparative poetics, and the study of contact and transfer.

How we write the history of children's literature, and our appraisal of individual writers, is shaped by national differences. Helene Høyrup offers the following reading of Hans Christian Andersen's reception both in an Anglo-American context and in his native Denmark:

> in the Anglo-American context Andersen's contribution to literature, such as his techniques of alienation, emphasizing that the function of art is to estrange us from our standard perceptions, have not been fully appreciated. In a Danish context, on the other hand, it is not always recognized how Andersen's literary sophistication is to a high degree related to addressing the child (Høyrup 2017, 116).

Andersen, in short, is read more as a Romantic writer in the Anglo-American context but more as a modernist in Denmark.

National differences have stressed entirely different aesthetic achievements and shaped different literary histories.

There are also ways to work across national lines using monolingual comparisons, as Kiera Vaclavik, responding to O'Sullivan's work, notes:

> Her approach is insistently multilingual (and *Comparative Children's Literature* is itself translated from the original German). Yet several critics have made a persuasive case for monolingual comparison on the grounds that a single language can encompass a vast range of cultural contexts ... Its exclusion certainly seems to impoverish rather than enhance the field of children's literature. There are, for example, strong reasons for comparing works in French for young readers produced in Canada, Haiti, and France. In postcolonial situations, where language frequently constitutes part of the legacy of the colonial period, an openness to monolingual comparison is particularly important (Vaclavik, 2011, 205).

Once you have begun to think about a comparativist project of children's literature, there are many possible national, regional, and linguistic axes of comparison that can be developed.

There are rewards to be had from working both multilingually and monolingually. New histories of children's literature within specific national contexts are also making a contribution. One example among many is Mary Ann Farquhar's *Children's Literature in China: From Lu Xun to Mao Zedong* (2000), which focuses on post-Confucian children's literature as an instrument of the country's modernization, leading into the Cultural Revolution. Many scholars engage with the history of empire and children's literature in a postcolonial context; I will discuss postcolonial children's literature in more detail in Chapter 5. Here I will simply note that much contemporary literature emerges not from national frameworks but from diasporic experience; as we see, for example, from a work like *Akata Witch* (2011) by Nnedi Okorafor, which features a Nigerian-born but American-raised protagonist, Sunny, who returns to Nigeria and discovers her own magical ability. She is one of the 'Leopard people,' set apart from the non-magical 'Lambs.' 'Akata' is something of a derogatory term for African Americans in Nigeria, gesturing to some of the complex frictions that the book explores. Okorafor's book has been described as a 'Nigerian Harry Potter.' Rather than compare it to Rowling's blockbuster series, however, it is more revealing to consider how its inventive magical framework draws on the practices and beliefs of the Ekpe people, a Nigerian secret society.

Each national or transnational case offers a potentially fresh vision of how children's literature functions socially and politically. In thinking about ways that Children's Literature scholars might internationalize the field, there are as many possible comparative axes as countries, regions, and areas in the world.

Case study: Edward Lear, *A Book of Nonsense* (1846)

Kimberley Reynolds notes that nonsensical children's literature has 'challenged authority, released subversive energies, [and] refused to condescend and preach to readers ...' (Reynolds 2007, 10). Edward Lear's first collection of limericks, *A Book of Nonsense* (1846), offers this kind of disruption in its most extreme form. Like Lewis Carroll, Lear explored both the pleasures and the perils of a world turned upside down, explicitly eschewing any moralistic content. Characters like the 'Old Man on a hill,' for example, flout the mores of Victorian society:

> There was an Old Man on a hill, who seldom, if ever, stood still;
> He ran up and down, in his Grandmother's gown,
> Which adorned that Old Man on a hill
> (Lear [1846] 1875, 4).

These breaches of convention had a special appeal for Lear's initial audience; they can be read in part as a reaction to the strictures of Victorian propriety. The limericks, Ina Rae Hark notes, spoke to

> the deepest concerns of a highly ambivalent era, an era torn between a strict set of social conventions adopted to give order to incipient chaos and the restrictions to individual liberty which that arbitrary order entailed. The *Nonsense Books* not surprisingly appealed to many Victorian parents as much as to the children for whom they were ostensibly intended (Hark 1978, 113).

The emergence of an explicitly 'anti-didactic' subversive literature was, perhaps, as much a vicarious flouting of the strictures of adult life as a child's relish in subverting orderly behaviour.

At the same time that many of Lear's characters revel in their transgressions, we might question how free they really are to pursue their eccentricities. Sara Lodge claims that most of Lear's eccentrics do quite well: 'Sometimes, as many critics have noted, these eccentrics are "smashed" or "banged": but for the most part, their energies exceed those of the forces that endeavor to suppress them' (Lodge 2016, 77). For a poet credited with moving away from the moralistic 'cautionary tales' that preceded him, however, he presents some severe punishments for bad behaviour. Citing food historian Margaret Visser's comment about the limerick 'There was an Old Person of Buda'—'Manners, and table manners in particular, are no laughing matter'—Peter Robinson argues that Lear often establishes dire consequences for social transgressions (Robinson 2016, 125). This is the harsh fate of the Old Person of Buda:

> There was an Old Person of Buda, whose conduct grew ruder and ruder;
>
> Till at last, with a hammer, they silenced his clamour,
>
> By smashing that person from Buda
>
> (Lear [1846] 1875, 24).

It is hard to read the 'silencing' of 'his clamour' as anything but murder or intense violence. Perhaps Lear is parodying traditional cautionary tales, but he also reproduces their essential structure. A person deviates from acceptable behaviour and is then punished. Furthermore, there is not enough glee or archness or irony here to distance it adequately from traditional cautionary tales. Ultimately Lear oscillates between a point of view that preserves eccentrics intact and unapologetic, and one where they pay a terrible price for their oddness.

Speaking in formal terms, James Williams notices that Lear 'observes with close fidelity' the 'constraints of form and rhyme ... The rules of poetic form often resemble grown-up authority' (Williams 2016, 26). For John Rieder, the wild nonconformity of Lear's poetry is less a permanent state of affairs than an 'interlude'

> where the children in his audience find themselves metaphorically suspended from the conventional world but still secure in the reassurance of the nonsense world's finitude, its balance of imaginative possibility and formal limits, and the certainty that the game always comes to an end (Rieder 1998, 59).

There is room for experimentation, but it has limits, which are quickly revealed through the regularity of the poetic form. The tight limerick form reminds children that, as wild as things can get, there is still a pattern and order to their literature. Throughout much of its history, children's literature made similar gestures inviting children to experiment and take risks, with the game ultimately coming to an end.

At the same time that Lear looks backwards to the punitive moral tales of earlier children's literature he is also a precursor to the unsettled angst of much 20th century literature, even **absurdists** such as Ionesco and Beckett. Joyce Thomas picks up a certain eeriness in Lear's work: 'That protean characteristic of nonsense and its unpredictability account for much of the discomfort it evokes in us, a discomfort which is reinforced by the verse's various paradoxical tensions. A vague sense of disturbance, difficult to articulate, constitutes the ultimate effect of nonsense' (Thomas 1985, 121). Many characters in Lear's limericks, rather than celebrating their own oddness, find themselves bemused by it. Consider, for example, the first limerick in the book:

> There was an Old Man with a beard, who said, 'It is just as I feared!
>
> Two Owls and a Hen, four Larks and a Wren,
>
> Have all built their nests in my Beard!'
>
> (Lear [1846] 1875, 1).

Nothing is as it should be; the human and avian worlds are all tangled up. The poem is also strangely static; the old man does nothing to remedy the situation, and his reaction is a gentle alarm. Here Lear anticipates a children's literature that is less clear on what children should believe or understand, and more open to a state of continued confusion. The presence of these very different affective registers reveals how any given work of children's literature, in Lear's time and in ours, can simultaneously act as a force to license the imagination and one that reins in imagination's subversive energies.

3
CHILDREN'S LITERATURE AND THE POLITICAL

As I noted in my last chapter, children's literature has long been imagined as a way to transmit cultural, social, and political knowledge to young readers. Scholars continue to grapple with the relationship between children's literature and dominant economic, political, and social structures, including those that perpetuate inequalities. Children's literature has, in fact, often been understood as a cultural force that props up the dominant institutions of society. Other theorists, however, have regarded children's literature as one of the most promising spaces for cultural change and countercultural ferment. Despite the historical and ongoing conservative roots of children's literature, Kimberley Reynolds argues, it has also 'provided a space in which writers, illustrators, printers, and publishers have piloted ideas, experimented with voices, formats and media, played with conventions, and contested thinking about cultural norms, including those surrounding childhood, and how societies should be organised' (Reynolds 2007, 3). Does children's literature shore up the *status quo* or provide its young readers with the tools and the inspiration to tear it down?

The answers to these questions are as varied as works of children's literature themselves and the myriad historical contexts in which these works are produced and read. Contradictions inherent in the way we evaluate children's literature are well encapsulated by Reynolds's description of a 'curious and paradoxical cultural space ... simultaneously highly regulated and overlooked, orthodox and radical, didactic and subversive' (Reynolds 2007, 3). This contradictory vision animates my exploration of the relationship of children's literature to the political world in this chapter, as a space that includes both subversive and conservative elements.

Any examination of children's literature as a political force involves the question of **ideology**. Robyn McCallum and John Stephens provide an excellent definition of ideology:

> Ideologies are the systems of belief which are shared and used by a society to make sense of the world and which pervade the talk and behaviors of a community, and form the basis of the social representations and practices of group members (McCallum and Stephens 2011, 370).

Questions of ideology are so important for the study of children's literature because, as John Stephens notes, ideology includes

> morality and ethics, a sense of what is valuable in the culture's past (what a particular contemporary social formation regards as the culture's centrally important traditions), and aspirations about the present and the future (Stephens 1992, 3).

Ideology, then, is not so much a set of ideas but the prism through which we see the world; it is embedded in our social and educational institutions, including literature. To Étienne Balibar and Pierre Macherey, 'the literary text is a privileged operator in the concrete relations between the individual and ideology and in bourgeois society and ensures its reproduction' (Balibar and Macherey [1974] 1981, 96). In their 1974 essay, 'On Literature as an Ideological Form,' they describe literature not as 'the product of a mysterious "creation"' that 'falls from the heavens' but rather the product of social practice (rather a particular social practice); neither is it an 'imaginary' activity, albeit it produces imaginary effects, but inescapably part of a material process ... (Balibar and Macherey [1974] 1981, 82).

Scholars in the field have grappled with the ideological impact of children's literature on young readers. McCallum observes that 'an individual's consciousness is formed in dialogue with others and with the discourses constituting the society and culture s/he inhabits' and that this 'subjectivity is always shaped by social ideologies' (McCallum 1999, 3).

While she views young subjectivities as shaped by social ideologies, McCallum is also interested in the ways texts 'can allow for a wide range of reading strategies and skills for inscribing experiences in the world with meaning,' allowing for 'a questioning of conventional notions of selfhood, meaning and history' (McCallum 1999, 259). Like many Children's Literature scholars interested in young people's reading, she draws on Bahktin's theories of **heteroglossia**—or the 'many voices' that a text can contain—to explore how such texts can allow for a questioning position towards the 'selfhood, meaning, and history' that constitute ideology, because they invite the reader into the process of sorting through their meaning.

In the next part of this chapter I will look at the role that children's literature has played in political and social movements, and ways in which children are addressed directly as social and political thinkers. While many political groups and subcultures earnestly hope to engage child readers with their ideas, others worry that children should not be burdened with 'political' content. Yet the argument that *all* representation is political, whether in its unconscious expression of ideology or through more explicit messages, has made a forceful impact on the discipline.

In thinking about how children's literature shapes children's understanding of the political and social world, scholars must reckon with the fundamental mysteries of what we cannot know about children's political engagement with texts. Building on my discussion of the reception of children's literature in Chapter 1, in this chapter I consider moments where child readers resist overt messages, especially heavily didactic ones, and how the field of Children's Literature is increasingly interested in registering and analysing children's resistant readings.

My case study for this chapter, the *Little House on the Prairie* series by Laura Ingalls Wilder, is an excellent example of a classic text whose overt political messages and unconscious ideologies have increasingly sparked critical re-evaluation. The series holds the status of a literary and cultural classic, with many readers sentimentally attached to it, yet its obvious racial prejudices against Native Americans and African Americans have caused many critics to argue that the books should be read more critically or abandoned altogether. Involved in its portrayal of Native Americans is the implication that western settlement was inevitable, which is an implicit defence of colonialism. The portrayal of the Ingalls family as a self-sufficient, close-knit family has influenced several generations of readers—and even policymakers—to espouse the values of limited government, a kind of unconscious argument against social welfare programmes that reflected the political ideals of Ingalls herself and also the strong libertarian principles of her daughter and editor, Rose Wilder Lane. In this case study we see how this series, which seems to be nothing more than the pioneering adventures of a warm and loving family, captures and shapes momentous events of American history. My case study ends with a brief consideration of a British counterpart to Ingalls: H.E. Marshall's *Our Island Story* (1905), a sweeping non-fiction history of England that, like Ingalls' work, is an exercise in building a national identity over time.

A paradoxical space

In the last chapter I noted that education in the classical period was structured to nurture and shape elites. Seth Lerer notes how subjugated classes of people were responsible for the creation and dissemination of children's literature in that era:

> Slaves were the omnipresent extras of Greek and, later, Roman life. Nursemaids were often slaves; so were many teachers. Aesop, that father of the fable, was himself a slave, and the fables and the tales that circulated of his own life are rife with stories of the servant who

> upsets the masters or the child who dupes the parents. Slavery is central to the history of children's literature, and it is nowhere more apparent than in classical antiquity. The *pedagogus* was the household servant who made sure the student made it to class and back. Well-born Roman children might have an entire entourage, from pedagogue to *capsarius* (the book-bag carrier). From miming figures out of fiction, children learned how to order others, how to affirm a superior place in the social and familial world (Lerer 2008, 19).

Paradoxically, children's literature from the classical period often stresses the triumph of the underdog. Aesop's own fables, as Victoria deRijke points out, were 'originally told as a form of resistance using risky humour to expose uncomfortable truths' (deRijke 2014, 49). Yet the overall literary and cultural system does not disturb the established order. The image of the *capsarius*, or book-bag carrier, is particularly poignant: he bears both a literal burden and the figurative one of advancing the system that keeps him at the bottom of the social ladder. In this example we see how children's literature as an institution bolsters the dominant culture even when the messages of children's literature itself are rebellious and subversive.

The establishment of the Religious Tract Society during the late 18th and early 19th centuries is another historic juncture where the expressed aims of children's literature stand in sharp contrast to its actual effects. While intended to redress economic imbalance by helping the poor better themselves through educative tracts, it served instead to reinforce the social hierarchies already in place, since the 'program of educating the poor was in fact a limited one' (Ang 2000, 13). As Kristine Moruzi notes of the 'waif novels' distributed by the society featuring destitute children, 'emotion and affect were used in conservative ways that suggested individual responsibility but failed to consider more radical social change. While encouraging child compassion, these texts nonetheless reinforce the social order in Britain' (Moruzi 2018, 49). Ultimately, one of its aims was to stave off revolutionary change or social upheavals like the French Revolution, stirring up charitable feelings towards impoverished individuals but discouraging a more thorough consideration of the systems that created and maintained poverty in the first place.

Much traditional children's literature has, in fact, been enthralled by the acquisition and maintenance of wealth and property, a fascination not lost on Perry Nodelman:

> The historical and ongoing relationships between the existence of [the middle class] and an economic system that puts a lot of value in the getting and keeping of property reveals another significant aspect of the subjectivity children's literature tends to construct and support (Nodelman 2008, 177).

'Golden age' children's literature, for example, is often geared towards middle- and upper-class children who, in the words of Susan Ang, 'had maids running around after them, came into diamond mines and earldoms, had holidays in the Lake District, owned their own boats ...' (Ang 2000, 16). Here children's literature reflects the existing class hierarchies and invites readers to fantasize about material wealth and privilege.

The cultural forces in late capitalism in our own era have raised pressing questions of children's ability to shape their own relation to literary and cultural products. As has been widely observed, capitalism is not just a strong force but one bound up in our everyday social relationships and institutions. David Hawkes argues that postmodernism is one of the 'many powerful and determined modes of thought' that 'seek to obscure' the contradictions between capital and labour in our time. This obfuscation—which he names as 'ideology'—happens because of the postmodernist disdain for dialectic thinking in favour of Derridean *différance*, 'a never-ending chain of deferred and displaced significance, as the element through which thought and history move' (Hawkes 2004, 14). For Hawkes, then, to understand that 'capital is objectified labour, that it stands in logical contradiction to human subjectivity activity, to life itself, is accurately to comprehend the dilemma of our epoch' (Hawkes 2004, 14). For some critics of children's literature, late capitalism (and the postmodernist ways of thought that bolster it) determines every aspect of children's experience of literature and culture, from its social institutions to its ways of thinking. This is also manifested as a concern about consumption and the demands of the consumer market, as we see in this lament by Jack Zipes: 'The difficulty is that [young people] will not be able to resist the constant pressure to conform to market demands and to retain their critical and creative perspectives' (Zipes 2001, 22).

When we see children's literature most fervently upholding the *status quo*, we might turn to questions of political affect to explain why. Ang, for example, speculates that 'the tone of authority discernable in certain children's books in the late eighteenth century up to the First World War' may have been 'intended to act as reassurance, and have been inspired by the need to combat doubt and anxiety caused by ideological and industrial upheavals' (Ang 2000, 13). Drawing on the work of J.S. Bratton, Ang avers that the growth of children's literature was developed in reaction to 'the increasing whirl of chaos (social, religious and so forth)' (Ang 2000, 13). Here we have a complex model of children's literature responding to both political realities and political moods. Thinking back to the work of Maria Edgeworth from the last chapter, a work such as 'The Purple Jar' could be read as an attempt to espouse clear moral guidance—a firm sense of adults knowing best—in an epoch of turmoil and roiling change.

Reassurance and calm that restore the existing order can be found even in contemporary children's literature. The rage of Max in Maurice Sendak's *Where the Wild Things Are* (1963) is the classic example, with his rollicking journey into the Kingdom of the Wild Things ending with a tranquil return home, and a 'still hot' supper waiting for him. Would the book have been so successful without the pacifying resolution and with an ending that kept Max in a state of adventure? Moreover, as Michelle Ann Abate notes, 'at the end of the book, Max's newfound agency, freedom, and even sovereign power are eliminated' (Abate 2016, 129). Roderick McGillis argues: 'What every society wants is a quiet and satisfied collection of people. Perhaps for this reason, many books for young children displace aggression and offer substitutes for desire' (McGillis 1996, 79). Perry Nodelman and Mavis Reimer note, for example, that much of children's literature is marked by a home-away-home pattern, where a protagonist might venture away from safety but return to the familiar and the domestic in the end (Nodelman and Reimer 2003, 197–

198). Adventurous, subversive children's literature often tempers its rebellious energies by the end of the story.

Where many children's literature critics see spaces of literal and affective safety and a return to familiar domestic spaces, others see children's literature as opening up a more subversive set of ideas and possibilities. Alison Lurie notes that 'the great majority' of children's books 'told me what grown-ups had decided I ought to know or believe about the world.' Her excitement was palpable when she discovered that

> there was another sort of children's literature ... These books ... recommended—even celebrated—daydreaming, disobedience, answering back, running away from home, and concealing one's private thoughts and feelings from unsympathetic grown-ups. They overturned adult pretensions and made fun of adult institutions, including school and family. In a word, they were subversive, just like many of the rhymes and jokes and games I learned on the school playground (Lurie 1990, ix–x).

For Lurie, this 'subversive' children's literature includes everything from Beatrix Potter's animal stories and her imaginative escape from her stifling family, to the fantasies of E. Nesbit, to the heroic characters of J.R.R. Tolkien and T.H. White. In comparing children's books to games and playground rhymes, she positions these works as a form of popular culture belonging to children.

Mikhail Bakhtin's analysis of the **carnivalesque** and the challenges it poses to dominant power structures has inspired Children's Literature critics interested in subversion. For example, John Stephens, following Bahktin's work on the carnivalesque inversion of order, notes three variations in post-1960s children's literature. Some books give children a respite from 'the habitual constraints of society' but restore normality at the end (Maurice Sendak's *Where the Wild Things Are* [1963]); some strive 'through gentle mockery to dismantle socially received ideas and replace them with their opposite' (Babette Cole's inversion of *Cinderella, Prince Cinders* [1987]); and some 'are endemically subversive of such things as social authority, received paradigms of behaviour and morality, and major literary genres associated with children's literature' (Jan Mark and Anthony Maitland's *Out of the Oven* [1986]) (Stephens 1992, 121). The rebelliousness of children's literature is charted here on a continuum, with some children's literature more oppositional than others. This taxonomy of degrees of rebellion is a good answer to the question of whether children's literature is innately radical or conservative; when it challenges the *status quo*, it does so to different degrees.

Ideology and children's literature

Children's and Young Adult author M.T. Anderson offers an example of a purely hypothetical board book for very young children containing only the following words: 'Up. Down. Farm. Town. Black. White. Day. Night.' This simple book, with its 'grinning cows, chickens settling down under blankets,' carries within it a number of cultural assumptions. In using several opposite pairings such as 'day' and 'night' it implies that the world should be understood primarily through binary oppositions. The cosy cows and chickens are part of 'a long association between young children and the American pastoral.' It is also a 'mythologized and de-historicized image of agricultural production' quite different from the gritty realities of industrialized farming (Anderson 2011, 372–373). Although 'Up. Down. Farm. Town' is a hypothetical children's book, it is clearly reminiscent of the many British children's books that idealize English rural life, such as Frances Hodgson Burnett's *The Secret Garden* (1911), which ascribes healing powers to the walled garden discovered by its child characters. Since child readers are in a phase of intense development—learning who they are, what subject positions they occupy—a book such as 'Up. Down. Farm. Town' offers a set of assumptions about the world that a person can understand as 'natural' and that work under the level of purposiveness and intention. Terry Eagleton points to this as he notes that ideology 'presents itself as an "Everybody knows that," a kind of anonymous universal truth' (Eagleton 1991, 20). The writer may not even be aware of the ideological categories he or she is adopting. Rather than depicting a set of economic and political choices that led to a particular system of food production, the idealized farm of 'Up. Down. Farm. Town' seems completely natural.

McCallum and Stephens note that children's literature can, and often does, hold overt political stances but covert ideological patterns are inevitably harder to discern:

> As the representation of ideologies becomes less apparent, the more desirable it becomes for readers to understand the textual processes that embed ideology within fiction, if reading is to be a critical process. The implicit presence of a writer's assumptions in a text arguably has a more powerful impact in so far as such assumptions may consist of values taken for granted in the society that produces and consumes the text, including children (McCallum and Stephens 2011, 361–362).

There are obvious challenges to the reader in understanding the covert, embedded form of ideology, because of a certain 'taken for grantedness.' We might also think here of Louis Althusser's notion of the **ideological state apparatus**, which includes churches, families, law, and education. Although ostensibly outside state control—unlike the violent **repressive state apparatus** of prisons, the army, the police, and so on—they nonetheless convey the state's values (Althusser [1968] 1970). For Althusser, ideology has no history; it is presumed to be natural since it works through all of the social institutions of the ideological state apparatus and serves to produce and reproduce social relations.

Eagleton notes of literary works: 'Like private property, the [work] thus appears as a "natural" object, typically denying the determinants of its productive process' (Eagleton 1976, 101). Given this ostensible naturalness, criticism's function 'is to refuse the spontaneous presence of the work—to deny that "naturalness" in order to make its real determinants appear' (Eagleton 1976, 101). Seemingly natural and inevitable cultural products are revealed as historically determined. While ideologies can be hard to combat because their 'naturalness' is hard to identify, they also shift over time. McCallum and Stephens describe how children's literature changes when ideologies change: 'Because ideologies evolve over time, there are ongoing developments in what children's fiction represents as desirable models of human personality, human behavior, interpersonal relationships, social organization, and ways of being in the world' (McCallum and

Stephens 2011, 368). Readers who bring fresh lived experience or a new critical sensibility to a given text can bring fresh awareness of a text's hidden assumptions.

Contemporary arbiters of children's literature—whether teachers, librarians, caregivers, reviewers, or literary critics—are particularly concerned with how we should regard older children's literature that expresses ideas now generally considered dated, taboo, or offensive. How should we engage with literary works whose 'morality and ethics' are no longer acceptable in contemporary society because they include ideas rooted in racism, sexism, homophobia, or **ableism** (discrimination in favour of able-bodied people)? A reader's affection for a 'classic' literary text might stand in conflict with that same reader's objections to the ideologies and values of the text.

Some publishers have re-released books with revisions that, in Clare Bradford's words, 'typically involve the removal of offensive descriptions of colonized or enslaved groups and individuals,' citing as examples Helen Bannerman's *Little Black Sambo* (1899) and the removal of the 'n-word' from Mark Twain's *Adventures of Huckleberry Finn* (1884) (Bradford 2010, 43). For Bradford, this kind of editorial adjustment is not adequate: 'What tends to be overlooked in such revisions, however, is that colonial and racist ideologies are commonly encoded in structural, semantic, and narrative features which are not ameliorated merely through the removal of words or phrases' (Bradford 2010, 43). Rather than ban or bowdlerize books like Hugh Lofting's *The Story of Doctor Dolittle* (1920), or Roald Dahl's *Charlie and the Chocolate Factory* (1964), Philip Nel argues that we should 'teach these books critically, helping students see the ways in which they reinforce racism, engaging them in difficult and painful, but sadly necessary conversations' (Nel 2017, 73–74). Not everyone agrees with Nel; indeed, there are many scholars who feel that books from the past with racist or otherwise offensive elements should be dropped from children's literature curricula and reading lists entirely, even if they stop short of explicitly banning these books. There is no 'one size fits all' solution to this conundrum, but one that will need to be negotiated by both instructors and students in the field.

Children's literature and political movements

C. John Sommerville was speaking of the radical Puritan movement when he noted that '[w]hen people organized for change ... it is never long before they recognize that the rising generation will be crucial to their enterprise ... Also, the image of the child will inevitably figure in the movement's ideology, because all such ideologies include a particular understanding of human nature' (Sommerville 1992, 10). But Sommerville could have been speaking of almost any of the political movements that see children's books as a way to reach out to the younger generation and cultivate their sympathies. Julia L. Mickenberg contends that 'nearly every social movement of the modern era, from abolitionism to socialism, communism, civil rights, Black Power, feminism, environmentalism, and gay liberation' was affiliated with a form of 'radical children's literature' (Mickenberg 2017).

The studies that have emerged of children's literature's engagement with political movements have offered an intriguing glimpse of how children's literature can function to influence young people's political views and sensibilities. Mickenberg's *Learning from the Left: Children's Literature, the Cold War, and Radical Politics in the United States* (2006) focuses on leftist writers from 1920 to the late 1960s, with particular insight into Cold War children's literature. Many left-leaning authors turned to children's literature when mainstream publishing and distribution became hostile to them due to blacklisting or greylisting. Leftist writers made significant contributions to non-fiction genres such as history, science, and technology as well as works that foregrounded the cultural contributions of African Americans, working-class people, and women. In *Left Out: The Forgotten Tradition of Radical Publishing for Children in Britain 1910–1949* (2016), Kimberley Reynolds noted how left-wing politics, progressive education, and avant-garde art were all entwined in works such as Geoffrey Trease's *Bows Against the Barons* (1934), which is based on the legend of Robin Hood. Told from the viewpoint of Dickon, a peasant boy who joins Robin Hood's outlaws in an uprising against the feudal lords, it portrays Robin Hood as a hero of the radical left.

The American conservative movement and 'right-wing' children's literature also produced a corpus of children's literature, as explored by Michelle Ann Abate in her book *Raising Your Kids Right: Children's Literature and American Political Conservatism* (2010). William J. Bennett's successful *The Book of Virtues: A Treasury of Great Moral Stories* (1993) is a well-known example of conservative children's literature: an anthology of classic children's literature that espouse timeless values such as compassion, thrift, and loyalty. At first glance, values such as 'thrift' and 'loyalty' seem like they should transcend partisan divisions, and Bennett argues that they do. But his production of this anthology conveyed a deliberately partisan message, implying that more 'liberal' children's literature, with its focus on diversity, had abdicated from its cultural function to morally educate young people. In Abate's view, the conservative movement in children's literature reflected 'a desire to roll back the transformations to American family life and morality during the 1990s that were precipitated by events like the successes of second-wave feminism, the advent of multiculturalism, and the rise of the LGBTQ movement' (Abate 2010, 22).

If Abate's more recent book, *The Big Smallness: Niche Marketing, the American Culture Wars, and the New Children's Literature* (2016), is any indication, the contemporary publishing landscape today has become even more complex (and arguably more chaotic), transcending the concerns of left and right to cover a 'wide array of personal, political, familial, cultural, biological, and psychological issues.' These include **niche publications** that deal with countless topics, including plastic surgery, the 'open carry' of firearms, and the proposed legalization of marijuana among other concerns (Abate 2016, 19). Desktop publishing and the promotional and distribution power of the internet make niche publishing possible, fuelled as well by 'the tremendous national divisiveness over contentious socio-political issues …' (Abate 2016, 2–3). In a world marked by disagreement and market fragmentation, it is perhaps not surprising that the traditional distinctions of the left and right might no longer apply to a huge array of cultural production.

In some ways, niche publishing is a refreshing reaction to the fact that children's publishing is increasingly consolidated in the hands of a few multinational companies. Yet niche publishing is not a challenge to market forms of production, but a profitable reinvention of it as a means to attract potentially lucrative niche audiences. Abate's study reminds us of the proliferation of ideologies as they are embedded within contemporary children's literature. Her work on niche publishing is also an important contribution to the debate about whether children's literature is innately conservative or radical, because it points to a publishing landscape which includes every possible 'special interest' and a range of political proclivities that inform the ideological infrastructure of the genre.

Being political

Many adults express unease about the idea of exposing children to political ideas in children's literature, so much so that in 2014 the *New York Times* staged a forum in its 'Room to Debate' section on the topic 'Should Children's Literature Be Political?' In her contribution to the forum, Claudia Mills argued that there was no such thing as a children's literature that was *not* political. For example, if an author writes about a child who has 'two mommies,' that is a political act. But if an author writes about 'a traditional nuclear family' with a mother and father, 'that is also a political act' (Mills 2014). For many people, the choice to deliberately expose young people, even very young children, to political texts is not an optional choice but an inevitable part of their lives, as we see from Jabari Asim's argument that he wishes to expose his children to complicated and difficult issues early in life:

> The sooner my children and grandchildren—all African-American—can learn about what it means to be black in a society still riven by racist attitudes and the uneven application of justice, the better equipped they'll be to navigate it (Asim 2014).

Asim's awareness of the need to prepare his children for the difficult and unequal world they will inhabit reflects an ongoing tension in children's literature between what Peter Hollindale calls 'the adult-in-the-making' versus the 'child now' (Hollindale 1997, 16). We have seen such a polarity throughout the history of children's literature, sometimes with the romantic ideal of 'the child now' holding sway, sometimes with a stress on the 'adult-in-the-making,' and sometimes with a confused oscillation between them.

Divergent readings

Children's literature has been aligned with various political affiliations and causes; it also includes several books whose political leanings have been interpreted in widely divergent ways. Munro Leaf's *The Story of Ferdinand* (1936) is a case in point. A seemingly innocuous story about a young bull in Spain who refuses to fight in the bullring, its publication during the Spanish Civil War meant it was imbued with political significance. For example, in an attempt to imagine the readers of 1936–1937, who might see the book as Communist or anti-Fascist, Philip Nel points out that 'Ferdinand takes control of his own destiny by opposing the wishes of the "Fascist" bullfighting community' (Nel 2011). In his refusal to fight, Ferdinand could be seen as a pacifist; as Nel observes, 'No matter how much the bullfighters try to entice him, Ferdinand just sits and smells the flowers' (Nel 2011). However, we could read Ferdinand's refusal as a capitulation to the Fascists, since 'a failure to fight would mean certain victory by the Fascists' (Nel 2011). The author, however, in the time-honoured tradition of children's authors who deny political intent, insisted that *The Story of Ferdinand* contained no political content whatsoever. Some read the text as propaganda, and Adolf Hitler banned the book. Mahatma Gandhi, on the other hand, loved it. But, after the Second World War, Ferdinand's pacifism was deeply appealing, and Jella Lepman distributed millions of copies of the book to the children of post-war Europe as a way of persuading readers away from a mentality of violence and conflict (Silvey 2002, 351).

Ferdinand can also be read in many ways that depart entirely from the context of war and peace. The eminent American science fiction author Ursula K. LeGuin sees it as an 'animal satire' mocking human pomp and excess, albeit a 'sweet-natured' one 'which, when you come down to it, is almost as hard on humans as Swift is, but a great deal more hopeful than Orwell. And is there any other satire in the world that ends, with no irony at all, "He is very happy"?' (LeGuin 2004, 29). Ferdinand's gender nonconformity has been a source of much interest, as he eschews the masculinity of the bullfight in order to 'smell the flowers.' As Katie Sciurba notes, Ferdinand's gender variance not only sets him apart from his fellow bulls but 'makes him unworthy as a competitor and saves his life' (Sciurba 2017, 290).

Ferdinand has, in fact, served as a standard bearer for resistance to a wide variety of social norms. Journalist Bruce Handy looks beyond the 'Iberian setting' of the story to claim Ferdinand 'as a proud American refusenik in a continuum that begins with Bartleby, the Scrivener, or maybe Thoreau, and goes on to include Benjamin Braddock, the hero of "The Graduate," and, for younger audiences, Maurice Sendak's "Pierre," of "I don't care" fame' (Handy 2017b). Thus Ferdinand represents anyone who wants to follow their individual wishes rather than follow the dictates of others. It is fascinating to see the book variously interpreted as a partisan text, as an exploration of identity (including gender identity), and as a more universal narrative of resistance.

Any individual reader might have surprising responses to a work of children's literature; indeed, any work read in multiple national or regional contexts might provoke divergent responses. Hergé's (Georges Prosper Remi) notorious *Tintin au Congo* (1931) is a complex example. This book has been repeatedly condemned for its racist portrayal of the Congolese people, but Kiera Vaclavik focuses on the ways in which *Tintin au Congo* has been successful in the country in which it was set:

> A 1970s survey showed that Congolese readers had adopted Tintin as a national hero and regarded it an honor that Hergé chose to set his work in their country (Assouline 349). For others, the text was downright funny, affording opportunities to mock and to turn even the most derogatory sentiments back against their source ... (Vaclavik 2011, 207).

Congolese readers did not view themselves as the passive targets of racist European colonialist imaginings. Nancy Rose Hunt recounts that Blaise-Pascal Baruani, a Zairian in Brussels, told her that parents bought *Tintin au Congo* 'for their children if they can to show them the colonized world their parents once lived in and how Europeans imagined Congolese subjects' (Hunt 2002, 96). Of course, it is possible to imagine any number of different responses from readers, including one of deep affront. Sanghamitra Ganguly describes the 2007 campaign of Bienvenu Mbutu Mondondo, a Congolese citizen, who sought to have the books pulled from the shelves in Belgium due to racist content (Ganguly 2018, 106). The variation in reader response is one reason why critics are so eager to engage with individual readers, child and adult, and to consider the cross-cultural transmission of children's literature.

Propaganda

We have seen that children's literature is deeply entwined with a teaching function, that it always carries ideological content, and that it is often explicitly political. But when does a political text lapse into **propaganda**? A work can be termed 'propaganda' if it contains clearly biased information used to promote a point of view or political position. Bertrand Russell offers a resonant definition of propaganda as 'any attempt by means of persuasion, to enlist human beings in the service of one party to any dispute. It is thus distinguished from instruction by its motive, which is not the dissemination of knowledge but the generating of some kind of party feeling' (cited in Marlin 2013, 9). In the light of Russell's definition, even heavily didactic children's literature is not necessarily propaganda until it forsakes the intent to 'instruct' and instead seeks to 'enlist' its readers. Randal Marlin draws attention to propaganda's 'lack of concern for truth, failure to respect the autonomy of those with whom one communicates, promotion of self-serving ends, seeking control over others, etc …' (Marlin 2013, 7). Twentieth century totalitarian or authoritarian regimes like Nazi Germany, Communist East Germany, the Soviet Union, and the China of the Cultural Revolution have been the most obvious examples for scholars interested in the ways children's literature has been put to use by a nation, state, or party.

To scholars working on totalitarian regimes, an awareness of propaganda is particularly linked to the extreme degree in which children's literature was integrated into the goals of the state and/or the ruling party. With regards to Nazism, Christa Kamenetsky seems to believe that the didacticism far exceeded what had been seen before: 'With the rise of Nazism a didacticism was imposed upon children's literature for which there was also no equivalent in the past. The didactic trends of earlier times had served at least the moral and religious instruction of the individual child, but now literature and the child were both placed at the service of the State' (Kamenetsky 1984, 22–23). German folklore emerging from the Romantic movement was co-opted for Nazi purposes, and, in keeping with the ideology of the Third Reich, Nordic myths were represented in such a way as to assert a continuation of Nordic heroic traditions.

Children's literature produced in the Soviet Union espoused an all-encompassing devotion to the Soviet state and an unstinting enthusiasm for the national project of industrialization (O'Dell 1978). Before the advent of the restrictive aesthetics of Socialist Realism emerged in the 1930s, early Soviet picture-books for children advanced avant-garde aesthetics, many of which are appreciated by students of modernist art even today. Yet Evgeny Steiner explains that, in the years after the October Revolution, these sophisticated visual styles were explicitly intended to bolster the Soviet state: 'Sharp angles, dynamic composition, shifted axes, swiftly tilting verticals and horizontals—all this charged the emotions, pulled people forward, urged them to volunteer, to build that five-year plan in four' (Steiner 1999, xiii–xiv).

East German children's literature in the 20th century had to be explicitly loyal to the ruling socialist party, as Gabriele Thomson-Wohlgemuth notes:

> Children's literature was assigned the same role and therefore held the same status as literature written for adults. With children's minds being even more impressionable than those of adults, it was clear that the influence would be more effective and longer lasting. However, it was not only out of political and ideological motivation that children's literature received the same attention as adults. Another reason for its

> high status stems from the fact that in a socialist society children are
> seen as people with equal rights. Together with the abolition of the
> class system, differences between adults and children have also been
> removed (Thomson-Wohlgemuth 2003, 242).

Here propaganda is tied in with something many Childhood Studies scholars have tended to find positive and desirable: a claim for the relative equality of children. But this equality leaves them more vulnerable to works that require their acquiescence in a specific political party, rather than less so. The model of childhood, therefore, remains one of greater 'impressionability,' but, of course, the coercive power of the children's literature remains at the centre.

The manner in which the Chinese government absorbed children's literature into the state is a telling illustration of the way that children's literature can function as propaganda. Mary Ann Farquhar notes of the literature that emerged after Marxism reached China and the Chinese Communist Party was founded in 1921:

> Revolutionary children's literature was not divorced from the Chinese
> Revolution. Indeed, it joined hands with Communist politics, in an
> intimacy unparalleled in the history of modern children's literature, to
> fight for a revolution which was considered inevitable by the influential leftist writers in the thirties (Farquhar 1980, 61).

Xu Xu characterizes books of the Cultural Revolution as promoting 'the negation of the self and the acquisition of class consciousness through learning from workers and peasants' (Xu 2011, 388). Here we see both service to the state and an investment in curtailing the will of the individual child in order to reach collective goals: a marker of propaganda. If asked about the distinction between 'instructing' and 'enlisting' children raised above, we could indeed say it is a matter of degree rather than kind: the propagandist work aims at indoctrination rather than instruction, and leaves very little room for questioning or challenging a book's message. It is more than possible, of course, that when discussing propaganda a choice to focus on regimes such as Soviet Russia, Maoist China, and so on might be a way of naturalizing propagandist functions within the Western tradition. Many of the politically committed children's books I described earlier in this chapter, all of which emerge from Anglo-American political traditions of one kind or another, aim to stir up enthusiastic political and social commitments in their young readers. The line between 'instructing' and 'enlisting' a child might ultimately be more blurred than we would wish to think. At the same time, the field of Children's Literature is increasingly interested in children as resistant readers. In the next section I will consider sceptical child readers who refuse to be 'enlisted' into a particular cause or worldview, in keeping with the field's increased emphasis on child agency and children's voices.

Sceptical child readers

In her 'auto-bibliography' *One Child Reading*, Margaret Mackey offers a subtle account of childhood critical reading that emerged from her location in Newfoundland, Canada, then at the periphery of literary culture. There were a number of things that Mackay noticed in her predominantly British and American books that did not match up to her daily life in Newfoundland. Rather than find this discomforting, this mismatch between 'book conditions' and her lived experience offered her a critical distance that inspired a lifetime of sceptical reading.

> In the 1950s (as now), many beginning readers were poor, or non-WASP, or aligned with an immigrant culture rather than or as well as the North American mainstream, or not Christian, or not straight, or not white, or otherwise outside the standard established in our textual materials. I am sure many of these readers learned, as I did, that literacy came with a switch-off button: *normal daily understandings do not apply in this text*. Eventually such experience might develop into forms of resistant reading, but in my case at least, the first response was simply closer to a detached observation of disconnection: *book conditions apply from here on in* (Mackey 2016, 67).

Mackey has established a productive disjunction between text and life, and she can now question both. Her articulation of 'book conditions' is a useful critical tool, since it helps a reader avoid being interpolated into the ideologies of the text by underscoring the division between lived experience and textual representation. Texts, then, can be taken seriously but they do not have to be taken literally: a judgment of what is valid and true is ultimately located in the reader's own interpretive authority.

The resistance of child readers, especially to the explicit messages of children's texts, is perhaps one of the lesser used but most promising tools in understanding the effects of children's texts, with the understanding that collecting the reactions of individual readers can have the feel of an unrepresentative—even eccentric—sample of opinion. Readers can be stubbornly bent on their own interests to the extent that they miss any political valence of a work. On the other hand, it is that stubborn resistance to explicit political messages that is the source of so much interest. As an example of a surprising reaction from a child reader, Ian S. Marshall describes his son's response to Dr. Seuss's *The Lorax* (1971), in many ways the 'go to' text of environmental children's literature and one that has been nothing short of venerated by many for its critique of overdevelopment's destruction of the environment. Marshall's son Jacy, however, does not share the text's horror of runaway industrial activity:

> Jacy will patiently sit through the rising action of the opening pages, where a little boy ventures to the end of town, 'where the Gricklegrass grows,' to ask the Once-ler what happened to the Lorax. But once we get to the climax of the story, where the Super-Axe-Hacker cuts down the last Truffala Tree ... well, there's just no need to go any farther (Marshall 1996, 86).

Jacy's enthusiasm for the Super-Axe-Hacker—the tool used not only to cut a few trees but to decimate an entire Truffala forest—triggers a mild despair that the pro-environment message his father earnestly wanted to impart is being ignored. Jacy's reaction shows that readers can and do find their own pleasures and priorities in texts, even when faced with explicit directives, and that these cannot necessarily be predicted in advance or controlled. Children's books can also overlap with play, as children act out stories and remake them in different ways. Within this play, children can support or resist the text, or sharply diverge from the text's norms altogether.

The fact that individual readers are abundantly capable of reacting idiosyncratically to individual texts does not take away from their power to shape opinion. Children's literature can be seen not just to reflect culture, but to actively make culture. At the same time there is much promise in sceptical reactions and in critical literacy as tools to empower young readers. In the next section I will consider how recent critical responses to Laura Ingalls Wilder has offered new ways to think about a series once considered a bedrock of American children's literature.

Case study: Laura Ingalls Wilder and the *Little House* series

Laura Ingalls Wilder's *Little House* series of books are an important example of how ideology functions within historical fiction, not least because the books have been embraced as classics for so long. Written between 1932 and 1942, they sparked a well-known 1970s television show, movies, and a veritable trove of spin-off products such as cookbooks and quilting books. On the market today are several first-person accounts by women who sought out the physical locations depicted in the books and tried to recreate Laura's experiences, such as Kelly Kathleen Ferguson's *My Life as Laura: How I Searched for Laura Ingalls Wilder and Found Myself* (2011) and Wendy McClure's *The Wilder Life: My Adventures in the Lost World of Little House on the Prairie* (2011).

Despite their classic status in American life and letters, or perhaps because of it, critics have turned their attention to the ideas and ideologies promoted by the books, both overt and subtle. The series, and in particular *Little House on the Prairie*, has been interrogated for its depiction of Native American people, destined to be displaced by the white settlers, as savage and threatening figures. The fusion of conservative and libertarian ideas in the book, with its stress on the nuclear family and scorn for government intervention, has also attracted commentary. Finally, feminist critics have re-engaged with the book with a renewed awareness of the restrictive gender roles it encodes.

Clare Bradford argues that the prevalence of historical fiction in children's literature is bound up with its ideological work: 'to explain and interpret national histories—histories that involve invasion, conquest, violence, and assimilation' (Bradford 2007, 97). *Little House on the Prairie* (1935), which focuses on the Ingalls' life on the 'Indian frontier' in Kansas, 1869–1871, is an important example within the history of children's literature. Frances W. Kaye bluntly characterizes it as 'apology for the "ethnic cleansing" of the Great Plains' (Kaye 2000, 123). *Little House on the Prairie*, affirms Kaye, is a book that 'lulls us into believing that the dispossession of the Osage people from Kansas was sad but necessary and even "natural," like all losses of the innocence of childhood and other primitive ways of being' (Kaye 2000, 124). This is the well-known trope of the Vanishing American Indian, as seen in other works such as James Fennimore Cooper's *The Last of the Mohicans* (1826). It is, furthermore, 'the myth of the necessary tragedy, the fortunate fall, that arises when the determined farmer meets the nomadic wanderer, the tragedy played out in Judeo-Christian myth from the time of Jacob and Esau' (Kaye 2000, 126). As Kaye explains, the Ingalls were squatters on the Osage Diminished Reserve; they had no legal right to be there. Wilder's elegiac stance towards the Plains Indians in the *Little House* series has been read as one of rueful sympathy, pointing out that Pa, Laura's father, is respectful and admiring of Indians in the book, although her Ma expresses overtly racist attitudes. At the same time, Pa is quite clear he considers that the land belongs to his family and that the Osage people of Kansas must move further west to make room for them. Pa's assertion might remind us of Terry Eagleton's remarks about unjust acts, that they are 'counterbalanced by greater benefits, or that they are inevitable, or that they are not really injustices at all' (Eagleton 1991, 27).

While some Indians in the text are approvingly described as 'friendly,' the narrative portrays them as a threat to the Ingalls' safety:

> Those Indians were dirty and scowling and mean. They acted as if the house belonged to them. One of them looked through Ma's cupboard and took all the cornbread. The other took Pa's tobacco-pouch ... (Wilder 1935/1971, 233–234).

Although they take some goods, they leave the plough and the seeds for the next year's crop wrapped up in the family's furs, to their great relief. Yet the Ingalls remain aggrieved at their losses, even though as squatters they have themselves encroached on Osage territory and used resources that do not belong to them.

In 2013 Benjamin Lefebvre noted that objections to the portrayal of Aboriginal people from both Native and non-Native critics had not lessened its 'continued appeal and sales success,' and he pointed to 'an endless list of sequels, prequels, interquels, sidequels, abridgments, adaptations for television and stage, tourist sites, and biographical and historical studies that seek to solidify Wilder's role in the shaping of American literary history' (Lefebvre 2013, 177). In 2018, however, the Board of the Association for Library Service to Children (ALSC), a division of the American Library Association (ALA), changed the name of one of their major awards from the 'Laura Ingalls Wilder Award' to the 'Children's Literature Legacy Award' because Ingalls' 'works reflect dated cultural attitudes toward Indigenous people and people of color that contradict modern acceptance, celebration, and understanding of diverse communities.' The name change was greeted with both approval and dismay on social media, with critics viewing it as an erasure of Ingalls from the history of American children's literature. For its part, the ALSC/ALA argued that the name change did not imply that people should no longer teach Ingalls' work or that it should be removed from libraries and reading lists, but simply that the organization needed to acknowledge that the inclusive values of the award and the dated racial politics of the books were not aligned. In addition to the controversial portrayal of Native Americans, the ALSC/ALA was also critical of the portrayal of a racist 'minstrel show' in *Little Town on the Prairie* (1941), where townspeople dressed in blackface, including Laura's beloved Pa.

In recent years, critical and biographical scholarship has uncovered the role of Rose Wilder Lane, Laura's daughter, in the composition of the books. Lane was one of the forerunners of the American libertarian movement, along with Ayn Rand and others, which has traditionally been ferociously critical of government intervention in private property and in the lives of citizens. Laura Ingalls Wilder herself was critical of Franklin

Delano Roosevelt's New Deal and prone to exaggerate her family's isolated independence on the western frontier, even though they received help from neighbouring families and from the government for many of their needs (Fellman 2008; Woodside 2016). Anita Clair Fellman notes that in the *Little House* books a 'self-sufficient family, responsible for its own successes, manages to survive many challenging circumstances without the aid of the government.' Furthermore, that 'self-sufficiency is somehow tied to the admirable values of individual responsibility taught by the tight, cohesive, and loving family' (Fellman 2008, 251).

Fellman notes that the *Little House* books continue to have an impact on their readers, influencing libertarian and conservative thought: 'the two women had predicted many of the concerns of present-day opponents of the welfare state and advocates of the free market (Fellman 2008, 249). Here we have one of the signature attributes of ideology; it can operate on individuals and influence them, and that process seems almost unconscious. The Ingalls family seems vulnerable throughout the series, and the narrative encourages the reader to root for their survival. They endure a long journey, an attack of 'fever-n-ague' (malaria), and struggle to eke out some material prosperity against extraordinary odds. Laura's child-like point of view as the family struggles for survival might make it easy to forget the kinds of political models being espoused, one of settler colonialism and anti-government sentiment. Sara L. Schwebel articulates this effect of historical fiction:

> Typically, children's historical novels invite reader identification with the protagonist and his or her immediate family. This enables an intimate, visceral connection with the past, but it is also limiting. Throughout the colonial period and early republic, indigenous people were forcibly displaced to create 'free' western lands for pioneers to settle. These characters—as well as their contemporary removal—have traditionally been minimized in narratives of western settlement written for children. If a reader empathizes with a frontier protagonist, can she comprehend the experience of that woman's Native contemporaries? (Schwebel 2011, 3–4).

I have noted, of course, that readers are capable of resisting the ideological pull of a text in various ways. Indigenous scholars like Dennis McAuliffe, Jr, Debbie Reese and Waziyatawin have offered powerful critiques of the book. It would also be interesting to see how the text would appear to a child of any background who had studied a curriculum that offered an unvarnished view of the genocidal acts against Native people. Ideology will always shape children's literature, but reader reception can complicate how that ideology circulates.

The gender politics of the books are also complex. You could read them as a 'feminized' version of the traditionally masculinized frontier narrative; they also make room for gender nonconformity. Laura is a mildly rebellious girl whose high-spirited antics stand in contrast to her exemplary, even prim, sister Mary, and in opposition to her Ma's genteel and sometimes repressive ways. Yet, as Ann Romines notes, the gender roles solidify as the series continues: 'Laura's growing awareness of her own limits and duties as a woman brings new weight and sobriety to the Little House series in *The Long Winter*' (Romines 1990, 37). In this sense, a rebellious nature, once tamed, can shore up the *status quo*.

The *Little House* books have been iconic for many American readers, and appear to harken back to a 'simpler life.' But a close study reveals that the childlike innocence of the books cloaks a number of political and social ideologies. The ongoing role of the series will doubtless continue to stimulate debate about whether the books deserve to hold a central position in the American children's literature canon, especially because they reflect a settler colonialist mentality.

In terms of articulating a nationalist vision, it is interesting to compare the *Little House* series with a British work like H.E. (Henrietta Elizabeth) Marshall's non-fiction history *Our Island Story: A Child's History of England* (1905). *Our Island Story* was written in Australia at the height of the Edwardian empire, from the vantage point of someone remembering 'the old country.' Despite its status as a non-fiction history, Marshall emphasizes the book's mythic qualities: 'this is not a history lesson, but a story book' which includes 'fairy tales' that are part of England's lore (Marshall 1905, vi). For example, the book begins with Neptune the God giving his son Albion an island. Brutus, the Prince of Troy, later renames it Britannia. *Our Island Story* covers a vast swathe of the history of English and British history: rewriting Geoffrey of Monmouth, Bede, and Arthurian legends, drawing on plots from Shakespeare's history plays, and extending through to the recent Victorian empire. It emphasizes both the continuity of English identity from the ancient Britons and the forward march of progress: from Parliament and the rule of law to a romanticized vision of the union of England and Scotland in 1707 as voluntary, natural, and mutually beneficial.

Throughout the book there is a stress on the virtues of the native Britons and their heroic resistance to the Saxons, Romans, and Normans, with an admiring portrayal of the Iceni (British Celtic) queen Boadicea, who led an uprising against the occupying Romans in AD 60 or 61. In contrast, the wild Picts of Scotland in the late Iron Age and early medieval period, and the mutinous Indians of the colonial 19th century, are positioned as 'other' to the true Britons, and therefore worthy of either defeat or assimilation. As Samantha Frénée-Hutchins notes, Marshall is 'sympathetic towards the indigenous populations of the British colonies, but native communities were viewed as less civilized than the British' (Frénée-Hutchins 2016, 186). Both *Our Island Story* and *Little House on the Prairie* offer a vision of national consolidation: a 'national story' related to foundation and settlement. These ostensibly simple books demonstrate the subtle and overt ways in which children's literature becomes embedded in our national literary histories and the role that colonization plays in those histories. Children's Literature scholarship is able to look both at the text as an art object, and at its political and ideological history within literary tradition.

4
THEORIES AND METHODOLOGIES

Children's literature is at the centre of many urgent cultural concerns, such as those involving development and psychology, family and social structures, and diversity and equity. Because children's literature is thought to bear on these concerns and many others, scholars are continuously drawing on new scholarly methodologies to assess the impact that children's literature has on culture. In this chapter I will examine some of the new methods that are changing our understanding of children's literature. The first half of the chapter will look at **Childhood Studies** and **cognitive narratology** to assess their impact on the field, as **interdisciplinary** methodologies. Childhood Studies looks at how childhood is historically, socially, and politically constructed; these conceptions of childhood have profoundly shaped the literature produced by children. In turn, children's literature has shaped notions of childhood. Childhood Studies has also inspired an increased attention to the voices and perspectives of actual children, with a sensitivity to the rights of children. There is also a movement towards a model of Children's Literature study that involves children as participants and shapers of knowledge. Cognitive narratology concerns itself with the intellectual capacities that young people bring to their readings of texts. It builds on insights from disciplines such as biology and neuroscience, and longstanding work on childhood development, raising questions about embodied knowledge, representation, perception, temporality, and memory.

The second half of the chapter will consider how attention to diversity in the field is transforming it. Thinking about race, gender, sexuality, and disability in children's literature suggests opportunities for social and political transformation in many spheres of human existence. Literary theory, activism, publishing trends, and authorial choices mutually influence this kind of cultural work. Work on race within children's literature, including the insights of Critical Race Studies, has illuminated the role of children's literature in constructing and maintaining racial hierarchies, with the particular objective of making children's publishing and scholarship more equitable and inclusive. Recent studies on gender and sexuality in children's literature consider how children's literature has developed along strictly gendered lines, and how recent children's literature has explored an expanded range of gender and sexual expression. Disability studies offer a sociological, political, historical, and cultural perspective on the portrayal of disability in children's literature as well as the social construction of the 'able-bodied.' All of these approaches invite a renewed understanding of the ways in which the field has traditionally excluded many people and sparked a re-evaluation of its most fundamental debates and assumptions.

My case study, Cece Bell's *El Deafo,* is an autobiographical novel (or slightly fictionalized memoir) that depicts the school experiences of a girl who copes with a profound hearing loss. *El Deafo* is interested in the whole life of its subject: her friendships, her burgeoning interest in boys, and her discovery of her own talents and strengths. The book can be productively illuminated by giving attention to theories about disability, gender, and child agency, as Wendy Smith-D'Arezzo and Janine Holc contend when they note that *El Deafo* 'brings new approaches in critical disability studies to literature for children, and contributes to the movement in girlhood studies towards identifying girls as sources of insight, voice and power' (Smith-D'Arezzo and Holc 2016, 73).

The title refers to a superhero persona that Cece adopts, El Deafo, which offers her a form of imaginative empowerment and which she ultimately employs to connect socially with her classmates. *El Deafo* is an example of the ways in which autobiographical fiction or memoir can speak to wider cultural questions while remaining focused on one person's experience.

Cognitive narrative theory and Childhood Studies approaches

When applied to a children's literature context, the academic field variously termed 'Childhood Studies,' 'Children's Studies,' or 'Children and Youth Studies' adds to our knowledge of how children's literature both reflects and shapes the way we conceive of childhood. It considers the lived experience of children alongside the literature that is produced for them. This endeavour is fundamentally **interdisciplinary**, as sociologist Gertrud Lenzer explains when she notes that Childhood Studies brings 'carefully chosen knowledge of children from different studies to bear upon the class or category of children to students in a Liberal Arts course of learning' (Lenzer 2001, 183). Childhood Studies promises to break down existing disciplinary and conceptual boundaries. Anna Mae Duane argues, in fact, that Childhood Studies 'defies the easy divisions of biology and culture, body and book' (Duane 2013, 3). The Children's Literature scholar who works within a Childhood Studies framework looks beyond literary text to consider its function in the whole culture of childhood, and the ways in which the culture of childhood itself shapes the text.

'Childhood' as a cultural construction is of paramount interest for Children's Literature scholars. Karen Coats, for example, uses a Childhood Studies framework to describe tensions between three visions of childhood: a Romantic vision of childhood as the apex of sensation and delight; a post-Freudian 'modernist' vision which stresses development and the attainment of strength through maturation; and a 'postmodern' vision, where the child is surrounded by and immersed within a plethora of sometimes conflicting voices and influences (Coats 2001, 146). The very definition of what it means to be a child has shifted, often dramatically, and the age range defining childhood has changed with time and culture. The literature crafted in response to those changing visions has also shifted. The various theorizations of childhood that we saw in Chapter 2 comprise some examples, whether it involves Locke's emphasis on the blank slate (*tabula rasa*), Rousseau's fascination with the 'natural' child, or the modernist 'child mechanical' who is a creature not of a nostalgic past but a technologically innovative future.

Childhood Studies scholars have also considered fiction and poetry seeking to 'imaginatively reenter the world of childhood' by authors such as Charles Dickens, Marcel Proust, Dylan Thomas, and countless others (Travisano 2000, 26). Creative practice is often imagined as a way to bridge the gap between adults and children. Yet these literary imaginings of childhood add to our store of cultural imaginings about childhood, and become constructions of childhood in their own right. The Edenic childhood of Dylan Thomas's 'Fern Hill' (1945), for example, gives us a child deeply in tune with his surroundings as he visits his Aunt Annie's farm, 'young and easy under the apple boughs.' This expansive pleasure over his environment, and the relaxed control he exerts over it, ends as he leaves the state of childhood for adulthood. 'Fern Hill' contributes to the rhetorical creation of childhood as a space of joyful ease, fantasy, unselfconscious leisure, obliviousness to the constraints of time, and connection to nature. Anna Mae Duane calls such cultural constructions of childhood 'the rhetorical child,' as opposed to the 'historical child' (which describes actual children) (Duane 2013, 15).

Interrogating the myths we hold about childhood as a literary, cultural, and political ideal may seem quite different from studying and intervening in the lives of actual children. Responding to the question of whether research into children experiencing deprivation and poverty is more urgent than work on the 'rhetorical child,' Duane rejects the distinction altogether, arguing that 'this scholarly hierarchy falsely suggests that we can indeed separate actual subjects from our literary, cultural, and political notions about them' (Duane 2013, 16). For example, our cultural investment in individualist conceptions of autonomy leads us to think of children as dependent and vulnerable, which is 'a block to full engagement and full humanity' (Duane 2013, 16). We might also consider, for example, how the Romantic, ecstatic vision of childhood we see in Dylan Thomas contributes to our resolve to provide carefree and pleasurable encounters with the natural world for children. When we aspire to change or improve the lives of children, we also need to account for our own ideas about them, and Children's Literature scholars can help us understand the visions of childhood that literary texts put forward.

Childhood Studies also argues for an expanded role for children in knowledge production, articulated, for example, by John Wall's argument that 'Children should be empowered to help formulate research questions, contribute to academic and policy conferences, and take part in larger social and political processes' (Wall 2013, 70). Justyna Deszcz-Tryhubczak suggests that children should 'become peer researchers whose contribution to generating knowledge about what they read has an intrinsic value similar to insights offered by adult readers' (Deszcz-Tryhubczak 2016, 217). Children's voices have, to be sure, been incorporated in scholarship before, especially in the fields of education, media studies, and librarianship; I considered some of these efforts in my first chapter. Recent Childhood Studies work, however, proposes that young people be seen as complete equals in researching their literature. This might seem unrealistic or counter-intuitive to many people. It presumes that children are interested in becoming researchers in the field of Children's Literature and that they have time and energy to devote to such a study. It demands an institution where children and their contributions to knowledge are treated ethically and with respect, one where adults are willing and able to share their roles as knowledge-makers in the field with young people. These are very challenging conditions to meet, perhaps beyond the reach of the current academy. Yet such an approach, if it were to be pursued, could go some way to eroding the boundaries and inequities between children and adults. It would necessitate a profound transformation of our modes of knowledge production in the field, as well as a recalibration of the usual power differences between adults and children.

Childhood Studies sees childhood and its insights as potentially transformative for all human institutions. Wall, for example, advocates that Childhood Studies should emulate some of the ethical and epistemological advances of feminism, which he notes 'reconstructed ethical ideas, for both women and men, around new understandings of gender, agency, voice, power, narrative, care, and relationality.' He notes:

> Childism should similarly rearrange the ethical landscape around experiences such as age, temporality, growth, difference, imagination, and creativity (Wall 2013, 69).

He uses 'childism' differently from the way in which Peter Hunt uses it as we saw in Chapter 1, which might be described as 'trying to read from the perspective of a child.' Wall uses 'childism' to mean that our ethical life should be completely transformed by children's needs and perspectives. For Childhood Studies scholars such as Wall and others, children's literature is less a space of acculturation into adult values and more a space to explore what the world would look like if children's ontologies, needs, perceptions, and lived experiences were the dominant force in shaping culture. Children's Literature scholars working within a Childhood Studies framework are inspired to think about how the representations children encounter in children's literature affect their lives, and how a focus on children's actual needs and potentials could transform that literature.

Cognitive literary criticism

Throughout this book we have identified a concern with the gaps between child reader and adult producer of literature, as well as a desire to better understand the reading experiences of young people. Cognitive narratology promises to offer fresh insights into the cognitive capacities that young people bring to their readings of texts, as shaped both by biology and culture. It draws on understandings of childhood development and cognition from the disciplines of biology, neuroscience, and psychology, as well as child development.

Literary cognitive criticism in the field of Children's Literature is sometimes known as cognitive poetics or cognitive narratology. Alan Richardson characterizes it as 'an attempt on the part of scholars with many different aims and methods to bring literary studies into dialogue with the new sciences of mind and brain,' developing models 'for understanding subjectivity, agency, consciousness, language, and psychosocial development through critical engagement with the best contemporary work being produced in university departments of psychology, linguistics, neuroscience, and philosophy of mind' (Richardson 2006, 544).

Many critics turn to cognitive narratology to learn how child readers make meaning. For example, **schemas** and **scripts** assist 'readers in connecting fictional, vicarious knowledge with real-life knowledge as well as previous fictional knowledge' (Nikolajeva 2014, 4). Roberta Seelinger Trites notes that:

> critics who are aware of the significant role cognitive conceptualization plays in reading and interpreting literature for the young have the potential to recognize how heavily dependent on the brain's forms of shorthand, such as schemas and scripts, narratives are. Moreover, cognitive readings allow us to examine the role language and conceptualization play in creating larger cultural narratives that influence the epistemology and ontology of youth (Trites 2014, 148).

Also influential in cognitive narratology as applied to children's literature is Mark Turner and Gilles Fauconnier's idea of **blending**, which places 'greater emphasis on the productive character of metaphorical and other conceptual mapping strategies, paying attention to the emergent ideas that arise from a given blend' (Richardson 2006, 547). Cognitive critics are interested in how the brain makes sense of different ideas, and also how metaphors blend different concepts together to make new ideas.

Can recent brain research actually help literary scholars understand more about children and their reading? In 2014 Maria Nikolajeva expressed optimism about the field's achievements to date:

> As a cross-disciplinary field, cognitive criticism has equipped literary scholars with new insights and analytical models, while it has also made cognitive psychologists aware of the potential of fiction as evidence for human cognition. Literary critics seem to be fascinated by the new vistas opened through recent brain research, confirming

arguments which previously relied heavily on intuition. But they are also confident that their psychology colleagues can benefit from examination of the arts (Nikolajeva 2014, 5).

Mainstream cognitive literary studies, however, have not been as interested in child readers, 'although some children's classics have been used as exemplars' (Bullen, Moruzi, and Smith 2018, 7). Nikolajeva points out that the study of 'brain processes during fiction reading' has been completed only on adults to date (Nikolajeva 2014, 7). The question of how much cognitive literary studies need to be based on empirical studies of cognition is an interesting one, and, as Bettina Kümmerling-Meibauer and Jörg Meibauer note, several models of the field are restricted in terms of the 'certain aspects of cognition to be observed – for example, metaphor or frames and scripts.' In their own work on picturebooks, they prefer to 'stick to the results of those sciences which devote themselves to the study of children's cognitive development,' including 'developmental psychology' but also 'disciplines such as linguistics, epistemology, and the study of emotion and vision that contribute to a comprehensive theory of children's cognitive development' (Kümmerling-Meibauer and Meibauer 2013, 144). Cognitive literary study doubtless benefits both from studies focusing on metaphors, frames, and scripts, and those that draw on empirical studies of children's cognitive development.

Cognitive narratology can offer insights into the ways in which children make sense of the world and the ways in which texts are structured to facilitate that sensemaking. But it can also underscore the cognitive and experiential differences between children and adults. Nikolajeva states this bluntly: 'Children's literature is a unique literary mode in that the sender and the receiver of the text are by definition on different cognitive levels' (Nikolajeva 2014, 13). A focus on the different cognitive levels of adults and children may, once again, draw a wedge between readers of different ages. On the other hand, the field can make use of the enormous body of work about child development already available to consider children as readers who are growing in sophistication.

Affect theory has emerged alongside cognitive theory as a fruitful method for the study of children's literature. Cognitive theory often encompasses questions of affect in that it is interested in 'the often unconscious mental and affective processes readers use to understand texts and each other' (Bullen, Moruzi and Smith 2018, 6). In the words of Elizabeth Bullen, Kristine Moruzi and Michelle J. Smith, affect theory offers a 'catalyst for new ways of thinking about the body, cognition, subjectivity, society, ideology, and texts …' (Bullen, Moruzi and Smith 2018, 2). The fact that cognitive theory and affect theory are both making their presence felt in Children's Literature testifies to the ways in which thinking and feeling are understood as entwined and mutually dependent processes. Nikolajeva notes that 'cognitive criticism, supported by neuroscience, has shown that the brain, through recently discovered mirror neurons, reacts to fictional worlds (descriptions, events, characters) as if they were real' (Nikolajeva 2014, 8). Bullen, Moruzi, and Smith believe that children's texts are 'used as tools for emotional socialization, enculturation, political persuasion, and moral or ethical education' (Bullen, Moruzi and Smith 2018, 2). In this vein, Marek C. Oziewicz has looked at cultural and cognitive scripts for models of justice in imaginary worlds and speculative fiction: from the retributive justice of an 'eye for an eye' to what he terms Open Justice, which views justice unfolding across physical and social differences, and with a sensitivity to individual environments (Oziewicz 2015).

Fascinating work on **empathy**, following on from the studies of Suzanne Keen and others, helps us consider whether children's literature facilitates insight into another person's thoughts and feelings, and encourages readers to share those feelings. Many people still think of children's literature as fostering empathy, as the many lesson plans and reading lists on this topic would indicate. Literary works are believed to help children think outside of their own situation, attending to other people's experiences with both heart and mind. How fully, however, does that emotional response translate into action in the world? Kerry Mallan argues that 'fiction that engages a reader with the emotional plight of a character does not necessarily translate into actions in the real world towards people who are similarly suffering, marginalized, or victimized' (Mallan 2013, 106). This is perhaps true, but it is useful to think back to the 'mirror neurons' mentioned by Nikolajeva above, which cause readers to respond to fictional texts as if they were real (Nikolajeva 2014, 8). It is perhaps premature to discount the reactions of young people to some of their fictional texts and the potential for these texts to inspire greater social and political awareness and action.

An emphasis on cognitive and affective development, especially if combined with a set of protocols connected to 'normal' development, might lend itself to a normative ideal of child and adolescent development, one that fails to take account of **neurodiversity**: the many different ways in which cognition and perception are experienced by an individual reader, including conditions such as autism, ADHD, dyslexia, and others. Yet the conversation between cognitive narratology, affect theory, and disability studies has the potential to yield helpful insights into differences of perception, embodied cognition, and emotional states. Mark Haddon's *The Curious Incident of the Dog in the Night-time* (2003), a detective novel where a young boy investigates the mysterious death of his neighbour's dog and untangles his fraught family history, is read as the portrayal of a character on the autism spectrum, given the protagonist's thought and language patterns, particularly his verbal repetition, difficulties with social interaction, and obsession with detail. Problems arise when it is meant to stand in 'as a singular representative for autistic experience' (Tougaw 2018, 128). Jason Tougaw considers the book as a case study in 'the tensions between aesthetics and ethics—or form and politics—that ensue when a novelist crafts a voice composed of symptoms of a neurological syndrome' (Tougaw 2018, 121). After studying reviews of the book, including those by people with autism, he concludes that the novel both 'dramatizes the destigmatization of neurological difference' and 'perpetuates stereotypes and circulates misinformation when Christopher is read as a singular representative for autistic experience' (Tougaw 2018, 128). Tougaw advocates that debates about the politics and aesthetics of the representation of neurodiversity be foregrounded when the book is taught. This is an exemplary approach to many of the challenges of cognitive theory and affect theory as they bear on children's literature, since many of the questions of embodiment and cognition in the field continue to be unresolved. The field will change as it responds to new research in the sciences and humanities, as well as to cultural change. Cognitive narrative criticism and affect theory inspire reflection on how children's minds, bodies, and affective processes shape their experiences as readers, and stimulate advocacy, both inside and outside the academy, for books that represent cognitive differences with accuracy and genuine understanding.

Diversity

In her essay 'Mirrors, Windows, and Sliding Doors' (1990), Rudine Sims Bishop describes children's reading using the metaphors of 'windows' (where readers can look into both familiar and unfamiliar lives), 'mirrors' (where books reflect a child back to him or herself), and 'sliding doors' (where children enter imaginatively into the world of a book). When young people from marginalized groups cannot find representations of themselves in books, or encounter images that are 'distorted, negative, or laughable,' Bishop writes, they 'learn a powerful lesson about how they are devalued in the society of which they are a part' (Bishop 1990, ix). Children from dominant social groups face a different problem: 'If they see only reflections of themselves, they will grow up with an exaggerated sense of their own importance and value in the world—a dangerous ethnocentrism' (Bishop 1990, xv).

Bishop's ideas have served as a rallying cry for scholars and activists in the field of publishing who seek more, and better, representation of children of colour, as well as other embodied and cultural differences such as gender, social class, disability, and queerness. The 'We Need Diverse Books' group is a non-profit organization that declares its vision as 'A world in which all children can see themselves in the pages of a book' (diversebooks. org). In his role as the Library of Congress's National Ambassador for Young People's Literature (2016–2017), Gene Luen Yang, himself a noted writer for children and young adults, issued a 'reading without walls' challenge to young people: to read books about characters who are different from you in appearance and experience, a topic you know nothing about, or a format (like the graphic novel or play) you have never tried. His challenge seems like one productive way to combat insular and ethnocentric reading practices.

The role of children's literature in upholding and perpetuating racism and white supremacy and its entanglement with empire has spurred new approaches which aim to foreground the voices of people of colour and to seek a **decolonization** of children's literature. Critics and authors have sought to articulate more expansive and flexible constructions of femininity, masculinity, and non-conforming gender identifications for all children and adolescents. A focus on sexuality has facilitated an examination of the ways in which books of the past have upheld **heterosexism** and **heteronormativity**; for example, fairy tale books that glorify passive female princesses and brave male characters, and that presume the union of a male prince and a female princess to the exclusion of all other bonds. At the same time, critics have searched children's books of the past for their articulation of queer desire and encouraged narratives of queer lives and queer community in contemporary works. The next sections of this chapter will explore the efforts of many scholars to reckon with problematic representation in children's literature and to seek a more inclusive publishing industry and scholarly community.

Race

Children's Literature scholarship has recently been invigorated by keen attention to race, with a focus on biased representations of marginalized communities as well as the under-representation of people of colour. The study of race within children's literature has, first of all, necessitated a reckoning with the ways in which traditional canonical children's literature has underpinned **Eurocentrism,** rooted in the white or European dominance over people of colour, and ideologies of white supremacy. Donnarae MacCann looks at how explicitly racist characterizations of African Americans in children's literature from 1830 from 1900 fed into systematic discrimination: 'By making Black children the brunt of racist humor, the mainstream's effort to discourage African American education through segregation, inadequate funding, short school terms, and other measures was given additional impetus' (MacCann 2001, 233–234). Robin Bernstein has studied how 'childhood innocence' was racialized in the 19th century, with white children increasingly associated with innocence and black children excluded from that innocence (Bernstein 2011a, 165). The subtler narrative structures that marginalize children of colour also have an effect. As one example of many, Frances W. Kaye notes the ways in which a 'secure and rhetorically powerful white author or reader' can 'turn the person of color into a perpetual victim or sidekick' (Kaye 2000, 126). Scholars consider these racist portrayals of the past, but are just as keenly interested in the ways in which these kinds of biased or distorting structures persist in the present.

The history of anti-racist work in the field of Children's Literature is in fact decades old. In the mid-20th century the Civil Rights era and Black Arts Movement promoted, in the words of Ebony Elizabeth Thomas, Debbie Reese, and Kathleen T. Horning, 'a bourgeois ideology of racial uplift' encouraging 'young people to lead the race politically and socially toward American ideals of progress and individual achievement,' which celebrated 'the victories and achievements of African Americans in spite of collective trauma and monumental odds' (Thomas, Reese and Horning 2016, 8).

The formation of the Council on Interracial Books for Children (CIBC) and the publication of Nancy Larrick's landmark article 'The All-White World of Children's Books (1965) in the *Saturday Review* (Capshaw 2011, 191) are other landmarks. The CIBC, founded in 1965, published the *Bulletin,* which sought to identify stereotypes, racial biases, and misrepresentations of history. Larrick's article brought attention to the under-representation of protagonists of colour in children's literature. A period of relative growth of writing by authors of colour in the 1970s was brought to an end by the disinvestment in progressive educational and social programmes of the 1980s, a situation lamented by noted children's book author Walter Dean Myers in his 1986 article for the *New York Times*: 'I Actually Thought We Would Revolutionize the Industry.'

In the 21st century there is a pressing sense that children's literature still has a long way to go in terms of diversity and equity. The Cooperative Children's Book Center in the USA, for example, reports that 37 percent of the US population are people of colour but that from 1994–2015 only 10 percent of children's books contained what they term 'multicultural content' (Lee and Low [2013]). In 2014 Walter Dean Myers wrote another article for the *New York Times,* entitled 'Where Are the People of Color in Children's Books?' (Myers 2014), and his son and frequent collaborator, Christopher Myers, published an article in the same issue: 'The Apartheid of Children's Literature.' Walter Dean Myers ended his article with the sobering reminder: 'There is work to be done' (Myers 2014).

In 2017 the Centre for Literacy in Primary Education (CLPE) looked at the books published in the UK and found that only 4 percent featured black and/or minority ethnic (BAME) characters, with just 1 percent featuring a BAME main character. Philip Nel identifies the 'considerable distance between mainstream children's publishing and the multicultural society in which we live' when he notes that writers of colour often have to seek small presses or self-publish (Nel 2017, 184). Publishers Lee & Low, who maintain a blog about diversity in children's literature, note that the majority of publishing staff and review journal staff are white, **cisgender** (meaning they identify with the biological sex which they were born with), heterosexual, and able-bodied/ without a disability, which might account at least in part for the lack of diversity in children's publishing. They pinpoint several areas where publishers can work towards better representation, such as making sure that all staff have a strong understanding and comprehensive training in issues surrounding diversity (Lee and Low, 2016).

The #OwnVoices hashtag on Twitter was inaugurated by Corinne Duyvis for books that feature a protagonist with a marginalized identity written by an author who shares that identity, as an attempt to encourage literary production that emerges from marginalized communities. Many diversity activists seek to encourage and support #OwnVoices writing as a way of combating the under-representation of marginalized groups within publishing. They also encourage authors writing about communities and identities to which they do not belong to take special care in their portrayals of what they have not directly experienced. Literary production has always relied on the representation of vicarious experience, as we see, for example, in Molly Bloom's rapturous soliloquy at the end of James Joyce's *Ulysses* (1922), which has often been praised as a powerful representation of a women's subjectivity evoked by a male writer. To restrict writers to what they know from their direct experience would be an impoverishment of the imaginative potential of literature. That being said, the #OwnVoices movement has been important in foregrounding some of the politics inherent in representation, so that stories of people from marginalized groups are not always being told by people from outside their communities. Writers who rely on vicarious experience are asked to be receptive to the feedback of members of marginalized groups, including critiques and objections.

The balance between freedom of expression and a community's autonomous control over its stories is, in fact, a delicate one. This is complicated by concerns that an over-reliance on 'authenticity' might lean 'toward the ahistorical, embracing the idea of pure identities untouched by modernity and globalization—or of identities that are singular in lineage' (Capshaw 2014, 246). What is hailed as the quintessence of authenticity by one cultural insider might not be greeted with the same spirit of recognition by another. In the process of creating a literary work, a writer from a marginalized community might do an excellent job of telling his or her own story but might produce a less authentic portrayal of another community, or appropriate cultural ideas and experiences that do not belong to him or her. None of this implies that authenticity is not worth striving for in children's literary texts, but rather that the intersection of literature and identity politics is always complex.

Anti-racist Children's Literature scholars have looked at patterns within the publishing industry that curtail the types of literature people of colour are encouraged to publish. For example, Katharine Capshaw decries an 'official multiculturalism' that demands 'the right story' of Civil Rights triumphs 'as the truth of black culture, easily consumed, for a young readership' (Capshaw 2014, 243). She adds: 'One might also think about the ways in which Latino/a, Jewish American, and Asian American texts have gravitated to topics of immigration and holidays in the 1990[s], sites that might serve official multiculturalism in similar ways' (Capshaw 2014, 244). Nel notes how the publishing world tends to steer Indigenous people and people of colour towards realistic genres, and in particular historical fiction (Nel 2017, 190–191). These genres are valuable, but writers, scholars, and activists have been calling for more diversity in fantastic and non-realist texts. In her scholarship on African American fantasy literature, Ebony Elizabeth Thomas identifies 'the success of new narratives from *Black Panther* in the Marvel Cinematic universe, the recent Hugo Awards won by N.K. Jemisin and Nnedi Okorafor, and the blossoming of Afrofuturistic and Black fantastic tales' as proof that 'all people need new mythologies: new "stories about stories"' (Thomas 2018, 8).

There have been several landmark studies of the achievements of people of color within the field of Children's Literature (Capshaw 2004; Martin 2004; Capshaw and Duane 2017; Aldama 2018). Some of this work involves looking at moments of intense cultural ferment, such as the children's literature that emerged from the Harlem Renaissance: the efflorescence of social, artistic, and intellectual productivity that took place in the 1920s in Harlem, New York. Capshaw notes how major writers of the Harlem Renaissance like Langston Hughes 'were deeply invested in the enterprise of building a black national identity through literary constructions of childhood' (Capshaw 2004, xiii). Langston Hughes, the iconic African American poet and novelist, published *The Dream Keeper* in 1932, his only book of poems for children. Poems such as 'The Negro Speaks of Rivers' and 'The Weary Blues' were influenced by black musical traditions such as spirituals and the blues, as well as scripture and prayer.

Work on race in Children's Literature has the potential to challenge and change our most fundamental definitions of children's literature. Marilisa Jiménez García argues that Anglo-centric and Eurocentric biases have determined our answers to fundamental questions such as 'What is childhood?' and 'What is children's literature?' (Jiménez García, 2017, 115). As the voices of writers of colour become central to the conversation, ideas about childhood and its literature are expanding. Jiménez García notes:

> It is important to recognize that people of color have been thinking about and creating children's literature since the forming of children's literature as an industry in the United States. Yet our scholarship seems to often forget and exclude these voices, along with scholars of color who have done the work to elevate the voices of people of color at the intersections of ethnic studies and literature for youth, particularly those in education and library science (Jiménez García 2017, 119–120).

Rather than being a mere 'elective' addition to the 'core' concerns of American culture, Jiménez García reveals that the literary and cultural work of people of colour has always been central to North American culture, and should be acknowledged as such. Her own work on children's literature of the Puerto Rican diaspora is a case in point:

> [T]he cultural and literary work of the Puerto Rican Diaspora community intersects with key literary and cultural movements in the formation of ideas about race, U.S. literature, transnationalism, and childhood, such as the development of library services and publishing for children in the United States, the Harlem Renaissance, the rise of ethnic youth protagonists and young adult novels, and the emergence of people of color on children's television (Jiménez García 2017, 117).

Work on race in Children's Literature involves a re-examination of the field's epistemologies and the scope of its inquiry. Addressing Children's Literature scholars, Jiménez García asks:

> What story does our scholarship tell about the communities and knowledges we value? Or is our scholarship centralizing only certain kinds of knowledge? (Jiménez García 2017, 117).

Work on race in Children's Literature helps us make sure that when we speak of 'children's literature' we mean the corpus of works that reflect the lived experiences of all children, not just white children. This cultural work is unfolding through the combined efforts of scholars, educators, activists, and publishers.

Gender and sexuality

Children's literature developed historically along gendered lines. M.O. Grenby (2008) acknowledges this when he notes that it might be more accurate to talk of a 'boys' literature and a girls' literature' as opposed to a 'children's literature' (Grenby 2008, 8). Critics have worked to account for these gendered traditions, and the ways in which children's literature has functioned as a space for young people to come to an understanding of their gender and sexual identities. Feminist work has been particularly vigorous over many decades, covering topics such as gender stereotyping, gender roles, male dominance in children's book authorship, and an **intersectional feminism** that, building on the ideas of legal scholar Kimberlé Crenshaw, acknowledges that oppression is shaped by race, class, disability, and sexuality (Paul 1987; Reynolds 1990; Clark and Higgonet 2000; Trites 2018).

Recent years have seen several compelling studies of girl readers. Sara K. Day has studied 'narrative intimacy' in the experiences of girl readers 'that reflect, model, and reimagine intimate interpersonal relationships through the disclosure of information and the experience of the story as a space that the narrator invites the reader to share' (Day 2013, 3). In *Out of this World: Why Literature Matters to Girls* (2004) Holly Blackford challenges the orthodoxy that women and girls identify primarily with female protagonists, using interviews with 33 girls from diverse backgrounds from the Bay Area and Philadelphia. When questioned, these girls repeatedly stressed that they wished to encounter protagonists who did *not* mirror them, which Blackford expresses as a desire to 'enter alterity' through a preference for omniscient narrators (as opposed to first-person narratives) and genre fiction like the Gothic (Blackford 2004, 29). While the search for **alterity** in reading might be seen as a way of meeting the 'Reading Without Walls' challenge issued by Gene Luen Yang above, because these specific girl readers prefer to explore experiences unfamiliar to them, one cannot help but wonder if their craving for 'alterity' emerges from a cultural expectation that girls should pay more attention to the experiences of other people than to their own. It is fascinating, however, to see girl readers standing up for their own readerly preferences. Anne Boyd Rioux points to the 19th century history of girls reading their brothers' books: 'If they had to remain at home in life, they didn't want to do so in their reading' (Rioux 2018, 169).

Scholars have also looked at the range of boyhoods that children's literature makes available, and their relationship to traditional masculinity. Here the perception that boys are falling behind their female peers in social adjustment and educational attainment, sometimes known as the 'boy crisis,' has a role to play. In her consideration of popular books for boys, Annette Wannamaker found that they were meant for a very specific audience: 'straight, white, middle-class boys struggling with hegemonic masculinity' (Wannamaker 2008, 8). She goes on to note that 'Gay boys, poor boys, and minority boys are often invisible in popular texts or, worse, are presented as the Other against which a protagonist's subjectivity is defined' (Wannamaker 2008, 8).

The narrative and literary possibilities for boy readers within mainstream children's literature, unfortunately, seem to be limited. As one example of many, Anne Boyd Rioux considers why *Little Women,* despite a history of appreciative male readers, including Theodore Roosevelt, is now almost exclusively associated with a female readership. She laments, 'Boys' distaste for girls' books, a product of the gender distinctions in everything from toys to books that children pick up very early, seems to arise as they discover that girls and everything associated with them are inferior' (Rioux 2018, 167–168). Her own experience of successfully teaching *Little Women* to male students shows that this is a barrier that can and should be surmounted. Part of that process is exposure to a broader range of books than those narrowly defined within gender categories. A book such as Adib Khorram's *Darius the Great is Not Okay* (2018) is an example of a text that might expand the possible narratives available to boys, with its portrayal of a tea-loving, nerdy hero Darius, a Persian-American boy who copes with depression, body image, and a strong suspicion that he does not live up to his father's expectations. When he travels to Iran to see his extended family he strikes up a tender friendship with a boy named Sohrab, which helps him to become more comfortable in his own skin, more able to embrace his own interests and passions in life, and less susceptible to the bullies at his school.

Despite the fact that children's literature overall has tended to reinforce conventional gender roles, scholars have also looked at how children's literature challenges these roles, overtly and subtly. Kenneth Kidd explains: 'If children's literature has heteronormative tendencies, which it assuredly does, it also homes all sorts of queerness' (Kidd 2011a, 185). Scholars are discovering queerness throughout the history of children's literature, including gender identities that challenge the male-female binary. For example, Susan Honeyman sees 'neuter' possibilities in *Peter Pan* and *Ozma of Oz,* with the girl Princess Ozma living during childhood as a boy named Tip. Honeyman notes: 'if not representing the *end* of gender, childhood at least makes a free space *before* gendering becomes imaginable ... In this light, romantic childhood can be seen as a theoretical precursor to the queer/postmodern *end* of gender' (Honeyman 2013, 168–169). We might also think of the 'tomboys' and 'sissy boys' of both classic and contemporary children's literature. Recent works explore **transgender, non-binary**, or **gender fluid** identities and expressions. Transgender people identify with a gender identity and/or expression different from the sex they were assigned at birth. Non-binary people do not identify as either a man or a woman, either because they identify as a man or woman at different times, consider themselves to be in-between the categories of man and woman, or define their gender as outside these categories altogether. Gender fluid people do not identify with any fixed identity.

Alex Gino's middle-grade novel *George* (2015) is a good example of a work that explores transgender identity. *George* features a transgender girl who yearns to play Charlotte in her class production of *Charlotte's Web* and who faces resistance from her teacher and classmates because they do not view her as female like Charlotte the spider: a friend stealthily assists her in taking the role for a performance of the play. By the end of the book the protagonist explains that her real name is Melissa and that she wishes to live fully as a girl. In a recent interview with journalist Neda Ulaby, Gino noted that the title *George* was shortened from *Girl George*, intended originally as a tribute to gender nonconforming 1980s pop star Boy George, but expressed considerable regret about calling the book *George*. That name was assigned to the protagonist at birth and is not her chosen name (Ulaby 2015). If publishing it now, Gino would title it *Melissa*. This is a good example of how the evolution of culture changes our understanding of what is important.

Children's Literature scholars have been considering the ways in which children's literature reflects queer sexuality as well as gender identity. The presence of sexuality in a book for young people is often cited by critics such as Anita Tarr and Roberta Seelinger Trites as a 'key determining factor between YA literature and preadolescent texts—if a book has sex in it, it's YA; if it doesn't, it's preadolescent' (Coats 2010, 322). That being said, there is increasing attentiveness to the question of childhood erotic and libidinal attachments, some of it inspired by Sigmund Freud's insights in the early 20th century concerning childhood sexuality. Speaking of Freud's work, Eric L. Tribunella notes: 'Whether or not one accepts Freud's account of the dynamics of childhood sexuality, his work is significant for calling attention to the erotics of children and to the ways that childhood erotics both do and do not mirror the erotic dynamics of later life' (Tribunella 2010, 32–33). Tribunella studies the many boy-and-his-dog stories in children's literature, reading them as a 'kind of prototypical romance of childhood, a transitional moment from parental attachments of early youth to the explicitly romantic and sexualized attachments of adolescence and adulthood' (Tribunella 2004, 156). He notes: 'Through the boy-dog relationship the boy can practice mobile and shifting social relations in a simplified field' (Tribunella 2004, 153). Yet, noting the frequency of death or sacrifice of dogs in works such as Jim Kjelgaard's *Big Red* (1945) or Fred Gipson's *Old Yeller* (1956), he senses that these exemplify 'a culturally widespread disciplinary device that involves promoting intense affectional attachments and then demanding their sacrifice as a way of (re)forming social subjects that are properly gendered and sexualized' (Tribunella 2004, 152). Having lost the dogs that they love so much, young boys in the American boy-and-his dog story are jarringly propelled into a heterosexual adulthood that requires a renunciation of the canine love objects of their youth.

Revisiting children's literary classics to uncover queer subtexts and relationships has revealed that 'many classics of Anglo-American children's literature are fundamentally homosocial, or concerned with same-sex friendships and family bonds. In retrospect, some of these classics seem decidedly queer' (Kidd 1998, 114). School stories like Thomas Hughes's *Tom Brown's Schooldays* (1857) were certainly charged with homoerotic desire, as were many adventure stories for boys (Clark 1996; Nelson 1998; Tribunella 2012). An emotionally charged friendship like that of Anne Shirley and Diana Barry in L.M. Montgomery's *Anne of Green Gables* (1908) is another example. L.M. Montgomery scholar Laura Robinson points out that, while Anne ultimately marries Gilbert Blythe, her most ardent emotions are reserved for female figures such as Diana or her friend Leslie Moore, whose beauty moves Anne to ecstasy (Robinson 2004).

While the classics have yielded insightful queer readings, there is also a distinct publishing market for gay and lesbian fiction, especially in the YA market, which is generally acknowledged to have emerged in the 1960s through 1980s with books such as John Donovan's *I'll Get There. It Better be Worth the Trip* (1969) and Nancy Garden's *Annie on My Mind* (1982). Early gay and lesbian works, like Donovan's, often had a melancholic attitude to queer sexuality and might even be termed 'tragi-queer' (Ellis 2018). More recent works have expanded the aesthetic and cultural possibilities for queer youth, with one landmark being David Levithan's *Boy Meets Boy* (2003). *Boy Meets Boy* offers a joyous vision of a high school that warmly embraces queer gender and sexual expression. The cheerleaders ride Harleys and the homecoming queen, Infinite Darlene, is also the head quarterback on the football team. Paul, the narrator, has been out of the closet since kindergarten, although his friend still faces opposition from religious parents. The book focuses on a romance between Paul and newcomer to the school Noah, with typical adolescent anxieties, and in its buoyant tone and overall optimism was considered a refreshing departure from the 'tragi-queer' narratives of the past.

While the expansion of queer children's literature and its aesthetic potential has been justly celebrated, we are now at a good stage to challenge growing orthodoxies around lesbian, gay, bisexual, transgender, questioning, or queer (LGBTQ+) literature, such as the reliance on narratives of 'coming out' to family and friends. Amanda Haertling Thein and Kate E. Kedley critique coming-out narratives 'because they insist on characters settling on definitive sexual identities as narrative resolution rather than allowing for the kinds of complex and/or unsettled sexual and gender identities that Queer Theory would suggest we all experience to one degree or another' (Thein and Kedley 2016, 6–7). Ryan Schey points out that 'not all communities in the United States or the world' would have used a model of coming out, with Caribbean and Latin American communities using a different model 'to manage queer identities and practices.'

> Scholars have variously named this phenomenon el secreto abierto, el secreto a voces, the open secret, or the public secret ... where people share a mutual public awareness of a person's non-heteronormativity but without explicitly naming it. Hence, there is a different relationship between visibility and the linguistic act of naming than in the Euro-US normative practice of coming out (Schey 2017, 37).

With this difference in mind, Schey calls for approaches to gender and sexuality

> that take seriously intersectionality as theorized by queer of color scholars. This is important for attending to the ways that homonormative and assimilationist discourses have offered some US students and teachers limited meaning-making resources for interpreting queer sexualities and genders, particularly those in communities of color, diasporas, and international contexts. When readers draw on more expansive and varied ways of knowing, they can more closely attend to the rich complexities that constitute the particularities of their own and others' lives (Schey 2017, 33).

This is not to say that the coming-out narrative is completely exhausted in LGBTQ+ children's literature, as the recent success of Becky Albertalli's *Simon vs. the Homo Sapiens Agenda* (2015), which centres on the main character's struggle to come out to family and friends, would indicate, even if the book mainly reflects the concerns of a white, middle-class boy with a largely supportive family. We might also think of a book like Sabina Khan's *The Loves and Lies of Rukhsana Ali* (2019), where the titular character deals with the challenge of coming out as a lesbian to her conservative parents. LGBTQ+ literature needs to be attentive to intersectional experience that expands the purview of queer children's and YA literature and challenges its core assumptions.

One of the most interesting strands in recent feminist and queer scholarship is in keeping with what Maria Nikolajeva calls the 'return to the body' in the study of children's literature (Nikolajeva 2016, 132). Over the past several decades, feminist and queer critics have argued that gender and sexual identity is largely constructed by **discourse**, which comprises the sum of social ideas and practices, including language and cultural representation.

However, after a long period of stressing the social construction of gender and sexuality, recent feminist and queer critical commentary has exhibited a new awareness of the embodied nature of gender and sexuality, as Roberta Seelinger Trites points out:

> We limit our thinking about humanity if we think of bodies as *only* discursive constructs. Undergoing puberty and making the transition from childhood to adulthood is an embodied experience, one usually emmeshed in gender issues. Whether teenagers identify as transgender, cisgender, agender, or gender fluid, biophysical changes in the body make it difficult to separate the lived experience of puberty from gender identification (Trites 2018, xvi).

This 'new materiality' opens up a number of possibilities for feminist and queer criticism attentive to embodied and sensate experience in children's literature. However, the interest in biophysical changes in the body and how they affect a character's understanding of their gender does not foreclose work on how gender and sexuality are also constructed in language and culture. In fact, children's literature is one shaping force for both gender identities and sexual desires, which is why publishers, activists, and scholars are so attentive to the ways in which gender and sexuality are represented in literature for young people.

Disability

Work on disability in Children's Literature has emerged from a sense that disability is 'a political identity, constructed in the same way that we now understand gender, race, and class to be constructed based on social norms' (Resene 2016, 95). Children's and young adult literature is a cultural space where social and political understandings of disability are shaped for a new generation. The urgency of this is clear when we consider Lennard J. Davis's argument that 'Disability is not an object—a woman with a cane—but a social process that intimately involves everyone who has a body and lives in the world of the senses' (Davis 1995, 2).

Disability itself is difficult to define. Legal, medical, and social definitions differ significantly. Legal definitions of disability pay attention to impairments that restrict or limit participation in daily activities and/or have a negative impact on quality of life. Medical definitions of disability tend to stress bodily or cognitive irregularities, which Kathy Saunders notes as 'a recognition that when compared to the majority of the population, a person experiences a difference in their physical, sensory, intellectual, emotional or psychological functioning' (Saunders 2004). The medical model tends to read disability as 'pathological,' even though many conditions that 'attract social consequences … do not involve ongoing illness or medical intervention' (Saunders 2004). Almost all disability scholars and activists prefer the 'social' definition of disability (sometimes called the **social model**) to the legal or medical, because it

> addresses the barriers to full participation in society caused by the practical, environmental, attitudinal or administrative framework of that society. A very simple example of the difference between the two is to consider a wheelchair user trying to gain access to a stepped entrance of a building. By the medical definition, the person is disabled by a medical condition that makes use of a wheelchair appropriate. By the social definition, the same person is disabled by the absence of ramps or lifts which allow the person to enter and proceed unhindered (Saunders 2004).

Disability studies allow us to understand children's literature not 'as a personalised, wholly biological and medically mediated characteristic' but as a 'social construction,' where plots 'both create and consolidate the attitudes and circumstances that are commonly found in contemporary society' (Saunders, 2004). While a full articulation of disability as socially created is rare in children's and YA literature, some texts pay attention to the ways in which social and infrastructural adaptations can transform the lives of disabled people. In Sharon Draper's *Out of My Mind* (2010), for example, a young girl with cerebral palsy has never spoken to her family and peers, and is presumed to lack intellectual ability. When she receives an accommodative technology—a machine that helps her speak—she excels academically, although she still struggles with social integration. Changes in the infrastructure around her have proved transformative, fundamentally changing what it means for her to be disabled.

Classic children's literature, especially from the 19th century, has shaped cultural understandings of disability in many ways, often stereotypically. Disabled characters in children's literature are often either villains or victims. For villainy, we need only look to Captain Hook in J.M. Barrie's *Peter Pan* and its many adaptations: his bodily difference is a major part of the fear he inspires. Disabled children in Victorian novels are often victims, the objects of explicit pity, as we might see, for example, in Charles Dickens' Tiny Tim in *A Christmas Carol* (1843). Many disabled characters in classic children's literature are caught up in an angelic death plot; like the fretful but gentle Beth in Louisa May Alcott's *Little Women*, whose unknown infirmities make her withdraw from social life. In several cultural imaginings, disabled children are conceived as unable to grow up. Other damaging stereotypes include the notion of the **supercrip**, where a character with a disability or illness is portrayed as having an extraordinary skill or genius that helps them 'overcome' their disability. In a study of non-fiction children's biographies of Helen Keller, for example, Peter Kunze notes how she is glorified as exceptional, which is typical of the ways in which disabled people are treated as 'courageous heroes who succeeded despite their "limitations"' (Kunze 2013, 306). With its traditions of 'inspirational' literature, children's literature might be even more prone to these kinds of idealized portrayals than literature for adults.

Disability is also used as a punitive plot device, one that brings young people into conformity with desired social roles. In Susan Coolidge's domestic novel *What Katy Did* (1872), for example, the tomboyish Katy Carr is temporarily disabled by an accident. As she slowly recovers she learns the virtues of patience (and the domestic arts) from her serene Cousin Helen, herself a disabled women. Disability tames Katy's gender nonconformity, and she becomes a more conventional, domestically minded woman (Keith 2001). Earlier didactic children's literature contains even more explicit punitive plots. For example, in Mary Jane Kilner's *The Adventures of a Pincushion* (1780) a young girl tells a lie and is then disabled by a horse kick, which the text traces directly to her dishonesty. Katy's experience, then, might be seen as a variation on narratives where disability is seen as a punishment for sin or social deviation.

David T. Mitchell and Sharon L. Snyder argue that many 'stories rely upon the potency of disability as a symbolic figure' but 'rarely take up disability as an experience of social or political dimensions' (Mitchell and Snyder 2000, 48). Instead, disability 'pervades literary narrative, first, as a stock feature of characterization and, second, as an opportunistic metaphorical device' (Mitchell and Snyder 2000, 47). They coined the phrase **narrative prosthesis** to indicate 'that disability has been used throughout history as a crutch upon which literary narratives lean for their representational power, disruptive potentiality, and analytical insight' (Mitchell and Snyder 2000, 49). Many works of children's literature, for example, focus on the emotional growth of a non-disabled character who comes to 'accept and understand' a disabled family member or peer, or acquires other social values such as courage or persistence. In such plots the disabled person functions as something of a prop or 'supporting player' for the non-disabled protagonist, denying disabled people their own trajectories of growth, something which could be traced back to a tendency to infantilize disabled people. Many representations of disability in children's literature, both in the past and in the present day, display the bias of **ableism**, which is the assumption that a non-disabled body is superior to a disabled one and that a disability requires a 'cure.' One of the most famous portrayals of a disabled person, both stereotypical and ableist, is the portrayal of Clara, a young girl in a wheelchair in Johanna Spyri's *Heidi* (1881). Miserable in the city, and consumed by anger, she is miraculously healed in Heidi's wholesome alpine setting. In Clara's anger and self-pity we see another destructive disability stereotype, with a disabled person acting as 'her own—and only—worst enemy,' unable to recover because of a negative attitude (Rubin and Strauss Watson 1987, 61). Clara's recovery is, first of all, medically unlikely, even impossible, yet all too common in classic children's literature. Nikolajeva affirms that these narratives of miraculous healing emerged when 'the young dead martyrs' of the late 19th century were no longer culturally acceptable, but both are 'dictated by the narratological demands of completeness: as an abnormality, a sick body must be either eliminated or repaired' (Nikolajeva 2016, 140).

Accuracy and authenticity in the portrayal of children's literature that foregrounds disability has been of ongoing concern to Children's Literature scholars; spreading inaccurate information about physical or cognitive disabilities can do active harm to people with disabilities. Barbara H. Baskin and Karen H. Harris divide unsatisfactory books into three major types: 'those that incorrectly describe symptomatology, treatment, or prognosis'; those 'that misrepresent societal conditions by distortion or omission'; and those where either disabled people or other characters exhibit 'highly improbable human behavior' (Baskin and Harris 1977, 50–51).

Terminology is often tricky, with some people—and fictional characters—comfortable with descriptions such as 'learning disability,' 'mood disorder,' 'girl in a wheelchair,' or 'mental illness.' Others are uncomfortable with, even offended by, these terms. Some children's and YA books explicitly discuss the issue of preferred terminology, as well as tackling moments where derogatory language about disability—words such as 'cripple,' 'spaz' or 'retard'—stigmatize disabled people, often in scenes where a child is bullied by his or her peers.

Children's and YA literature has a complex relationship with representing medical diagnoses directly in texts. In Sherman Alexie's novel *The Absolutely True Diary of a Part-Time Indian* (2007) we learn about the protagonist's hydrocephalus on the first page of the text. Some books delay diagnosis, such as R.J.

Palacio's *Wonder* (2012), where a chapter in the voice of Via, the sister of the protagonist Auggie Pullman, explains his facial difference as a result of mandibulofacial dysostosis, more commonly known as Treacher Collins Syndrome, after we have read a chapter in Auggie's voice, one without a medical diagnosis. Other books eschew diagnosis altogether. In Jack Gantos' *Joey Pigza Swallowed the Key* (1998), for example, we learn that Joey is often 'wired' and wears a medication patch, which might imply either ADD (attention deficit disorder) or ADHD (attention deficit hyperactivity disorder), but his condition is never named. The book does make a link between Joey's condition and his troubled home life; his family's dysfunction makes his treatment inconsistent and therefore less effective.

How does the presence, or absence, of diagnosis affect a reader's understanding of a character's disability? A candid diagnosis at the beginning of a text could be read as resistance to the stigma of 'withholding' medical information; a delayed diagnosis might be an attempt to explore the character before offering a medical perspective; and an avoidance of diagnosis can be seen as an attempt to downplay the medical dimensions of disability altogether. Michael Bérubé laments the over-reliance on diagnosis in literary disability studies: 'Disability studies need not and should not predicate its existence as a practice of criticism by reading a literary text in one hand and the DSM-5 in the other, even when a text explicitly announces that one or more of its characters is (for example) on the autism spectrum' (Bérubé 2016, 20). The DSM, or Diagnostic Standard Manual, is published by the American Psychiatric Association and offers diagnostic criteria for mental disorders. By offering the image of the critic reading a work of fiction largely in the light of the DSM, Bérubé is expressing concern that a complex literary character will be reduced to their clinical symptoms. Additionally, when a character is explicitly diagnosed in a text they might be considered only in the context of their disability.

The engagement between children's literature and disability studies has been productive, first of all for helping Children's Literature scholars understand how many classic books offer a distorted vision of disability. It has offered tools to think about the political role children's literature can play in creating political solidarities that seek to transform our cultural understandings of disability. It also shows that children's literature has immense representative power for those who share a given disability, and the promise of offering deeper understanding to those who do not. My case study, Cece Bell's *El Deafo*, offers a good example of a contemporary narrative that provides a window into one experience of disability while not claiming to speak for all deaf or hearing-impaired people.

Throughout this chapter we have seen how the publishing industry and individual writers have responded to developments in the scholarship around race, gender, sexuality, and disability, although such developments are often slow in nature and imperfect in their effects. In their turn, scholars are taking note of the conversations on social media and in the popular press around diversity, equity, and representation, and initiating those conversations themselves. We therefore see a loop between literature, scholarship, and politics, which testifies to the fact that Children's Literature is of urgent cultural concern in many sectors of society.

Case study: Cece Bell's *El Deafo*

Cece Bell's *El Deafo* (2014) is sometimes described as a 'slightly fictionalized' memoir, and at other times as an autobiographical graphic novel. It tells the story of Cece, a young girl growing up in the 1980s with a profound hearing loss, focusing on her experiences at school and her childhood friendships. The pictures are rendered in the style of cartoons, with captions and speech bubbles. The colourist for the book, David Lasky, drew on bright palettes reminiscent of 1970s' and 1980s' cartoons, such as those produced by the Hanna-Barbera studio. One of the most striking features of *El Deafo* is that the characters are depicted as rabbits, which inevitably draws the reader's attention to their long rabbit ears; as a child, Bell thought of herself as the only rabbit in school whose ears did not work properly.

Cece's disability is portrayed through *El Deafo*'s narrative but also in the visual depiction of her hearing aids; including the Phonic Ear, which consists of a large box connected to Cece's ears with prominent cords. The speech bubbles play a role in evoking deafness as well. Sometimes the words in the speech bubbles appear garbled on the page, like 'Jerry's mop' for 'cherry pop,' indicating that the hearing aid has helped Cece hear the sounds but she needs to lip-read before she can ascertain their proper meaning. Sometimes the words fade out in the speech bubble to show diminishing hearing, and sometimes speech bubbles appear entirely blank as the batteries for her hearing aid run down or as she shuts it off. As Sara Kersten and Ashley K. Dallacqua note, 'the constant visual reminder of the ears and the hearing aids' serve to emphasize that 'readers cannot forget this is a book about a girl with a hearing loss' (Kersten and Dallacqua 2017, 21). Yet Wendy Smith-D'Arezzo and Janine Holc contend that it is not Cece, but the hearing people around her, who fail 'in their attempts to make meaning' when they misunderstand her (Smith-D'Arezzo and Holc 2016, 73). The hearing people are the ones who lack the correct perceptions. The fact that Bell is a memoirist (or perhaps an autobiographical novelist) and this is an #OwnVoices story plays a large role in the narrative's focus on, and normalization of, Cece's experience.

The novel is equally interested in Cece's social development. For example, she learns to distance herself from her pushy, bullying friend Laura and to develop a genuine and sustained friendship with another girl, Martha. Bell uses the fantasy mode in the novel by using a superhero fantasy to explore her own shifting sense of powerlessness and empowerment. After seeing an after-school special on TV, where a character is addressed in a derogatory fashion as 'Deafo,' Cece creates a new persona for herself of 'El Deafo' (Bell 2014, 84). When she imagines 'El Deafo,' complete with a bold red cape, it is a means of vicariously taking power for herself in situations that are awkward or frustrating. El Deafo is often seen chastising or punishing Cece's social enemies. While this is a vision of child agency, it includes an element of isolation: 'Superheroes might be awesome but they are also different. And being different feels a lot like being alone' (Bell 2014, 46).

Cece does, however, draw on her 'El Deafo' persona to establish a connection with her classmates, and that is through sharing the capacities of the Phonic Ear, which connects to a microphone worn by Cece's teacher. When the teacher forgets to remove the microphone, Cece can overhear the teacher when she leaves the classroom, even in the bathroom, to her juvenile amusement and ultimately to that of her classmates. She summons up the courage to tell her first crush, Mike Miller, of her ability to hear the teacher all over the school ('I have an amazing ability ...') and he concocts a plan where Cece can warn the rowdy class when the teacher is returning to the classroom so they can appear innocently to have been quiet the whole time (Bell 2014, 201–202). She thus becomes a hero to her classmates.

In *El Deafo*, the character Cece refuses to learn American Sign Language and attends a mainstream school where she learns oral speech. Before the book was released, Bell was worried that this aspect would prove troubling to some members of the Deaf community. Many deaf people view their deafness as a positive difference and consider themselves part of the Deaf community (capital D), in contrast to others who consider their deafness (small d) as a disability, perhaps seeking cures. Members of the Deaf community generally seek to communicate through sign languages (like American Sign Language, British Sign Language, and many others). Cece does not wish to learn sign language and uses hearing aids and lip reading; her approach is quite different from those who rely on sign language and who see themselves as part of the Deaf community. Acknowledging the different positions in the d/Deaf community, Bell carefully crafted an afterword that acknowledged: 'I am an expert on no one's deafness but my own' (Bell 2014, n.p.). She explains that the experience of deafness varies significantly in terms of cause and severity, but most importantly in 'what a person might choose to do with his or her hearing loss' (Bell 2014, n.p).

The reception to *El Deafo* in the Deaf and Hard of Hearing (HoH) community has, in fact, been generally positive. Amanda Lee, a library media specialist at the Atlanta Area School for the Deaf, where the language used is American Sign Language, comments: 'I was curious how kids would respond to it. I had only one or two who said, "that's not me." The rest didn't care. It was a deaf person who has struggles like [the kids here have]. So much is universal to their experience' (Bayliss 2017). This kind of reliance on individual experience is reminiscent of the unique properties of memoir, or the autobiographical novel, which nonetheless has the capacity to engage readers who do not fully share the writer's experience. Returning to questions of diversity, it also points to the need for books that represent other forms of D/deafness, and the danger that arises when the field of Children's Literature settles on a single book that might be taken to represent all forms of deaf experience.

In this vein, Smith-D'Arezzo and Holc argue that *El Deafo* 'falls short in that it does not fully explore the racialized and classed implications of its female bodies. Cece's taken-for-granted whiteness and middle-class milieu point to a need for further critical analysis of stories about girls and for girls' (Smith-D'Arezzo and Holc 2016, 74). The book also does not engage with gender nonconformity or queer sexuality. Even if we appreciate a book's achievements in capturing the experience of disability in an accurate and authentic way, no single book can do full justice to the many facets of intersectional identity, which in this case includes race, class, and queer identity but could also involve other types of embodied and social difference. Genuine diversification of the field relies on a proliferation of individual stories that capture a wide range of experiences and identities.

5

CHILDREN'S LITERATURE AND THE GLOBAL AND NATURAL WORLD

Children's literature is tied to some of the 21st century's most pressing global challenges, including what it means to be human in a changing world. Children are imagined as the drivers of change and innovation, but as the denizens of the future they are also viewed as uniquely vulnerable to global threats such as violence, political upheaval, climate change, and other environmental disasters. Scholars draw on **postcolonial** criticism, **ecocriticism**, and **animal studies** to explore how children are educated about the world they will inherit and the challenges they will face in decades to come. Each of these approaches offers ways to think about global change, whether a matter of the **decolonization** of the field to honour **Indigenous** ways of knowing and living, or one of a renewed respect for the earth, through to a recalibration of the power dynamics between humans and animals. The human-animal relationship in children's literature is one of the most critical; not only because so many children's literary and cultural works feature animals but because children's literature, through a unique ability to make young readers imaginatively enter into the experience of animals, is capable of at least temporarily dethroning human beings as the pinnacle of evolution. Through the device of **anthropomorphism**, the humanization of animals, and the **fable form**, animals have served as a vehicle to explore human concerns, functioning as 'people in disguise.' Yet many contemporary writers for children and young adults imagine ways to consider animal destinies quite apart from human concerns. Animal studies emerges as a critical tool to think through ways of bringing human and animal lives into better harmony, as well as offering a certain candour about the threat that human intervention in animal lives poses to those lives, as we see in a work such as Richard Adams's *Watership Down* (1972). To understand the potential for a remade human-animal relationship is also to consider the ways in which people have exploited animals and the natural world.

Some of the most exciting conversations within Children's Literature are ignited when different critical approaches are brought into conversation for the first time. Texts about environmental degradation are often also about colonial exploitation, as seen from Susan L. Roth and Cindy Trumbore's *Parrots Over Puerto Rico* (2013), which explores how Puerto Rican parrots faced extinction in the 1960s because colonialism and foreign occupation destroyed much of their habitat. New critical lenses often inspire scholars to look at familiar texts in new ways, and they touch on our current cultural preoccupations. For example, ecocritical approaches and animal studies offer new insights into the hyper-canonical *Charlotte's Web*, especially in relation to the ways in which natural spaces function in the book and the complex human-animal dynamics that result. The engagement of children's literature with the environment, with non-human animals, and across national borders relates back to the questions about human relations I discussed in the last chapter and adds another dimension to new conversations about child-adult relations as children become involved in discussions about our weightiest cultural questions.

My case study for this chapter is Kate DiCamillo's *Flora and Ulysses: The Illuminated Adventures* (2013), a book about a deepening friendship between a girl (Flora) and a squirrel (Ulysses). Its premise, that a squirrel unexpectedly gains sentience and a penchant for poetry, is light and whimsical, but also—through Flora and Ulysses' love for each other—offers an imaginative attempt to bridge a seemingly impossible gap between people and animals. In the process the book does impose a critical consciousness on Ulysses, its animal character, but it also reflects a burgeoning cultural understanding that animals possess their own systems of knowledge and sentience. It also speaks to the possibility of healing fractured relations between people. At the beginning of the book Flora and her mother have a difficult relationship, fuelled in part by her mother's lack of acceptance of Flora's nonconformist reading interests and gender presentation. By the novel's end they reach a *rapprochement* that can be illuminated by new feminist models of the ethics of care and relationality, as well as the soothing of intergenerational tensions. *Flora and Ulysses* works in the fantasy mode but offers ways to think through pressing concerns of our contemporary moment. It imagines ways in which very different people and beings might come to a better understanding of each other.

Postcoloniality and globalization

Postcolonial approaches reckon with the legacies of **colonialism** in children's literature and seek to dismantle structures of imperialism in children's culture. Children's literature, whether consciously or unconsciously, has portrayed colonized people as 'others' in order to justify colonialism, the process by which a country attains control over another country, settling it, and exploiting it culturally and/or economically. Anglophone postcolonial children's literature tends to be concentrated on the British empire and its aftermath, with a focus on North America, Australia/New Zealand, India, and the Pacific. We might also think of non-Anglophone colonializing nations, such as Belgium with its *Tintin* books, or Jules Verne in France. Verne's *Cinq semaines en ballon* (1862) depicts a balloon trip from Zanzibar to the coast of Senegal and shows an Africa that 'was as much *terra incognita*, to be peopled with Europeans and European fantasies, as the Earth's core or the moon' (Dine 1997, 184).

Looking at children's literature within a postcolonial frame is complicated by a longstanding commonplace that children are themselves a colonized group, as expressed in the work of Perry Nodelman (1992), Roderick McGillis and Meena Khorana (1997), M. Daphne Kutzer (2000), and others. Since children are required to participate in and master a culture made *for* them and not *by* them, thinkers in this vein deem children to be colonized subjects. This is reminiscent of Jacqueline Rose's work, discussed in Chapter 1, which considers children's literature as a vehicle for the imposition of adult cultural concerns on children. Nodelman's essay, 'The Other: Orientalism, Colonialism, and Children's Literature' (1992), drew on Edward Said's concept of **Orientalism**, which pointed to the exoticized fantasies that Western scholars and travellers generated about Arab and Asian people in order to justify their colonial ventures. Nodelman argued that our representations of childhood shared similar structures, including 'inherent inferiority' (Nodelman 1992, 29).

Yet many postcolonial critics argue that describing *all* childhoods as 'colonialized' elides the experience of actual young people whose lives and political realities were, and remain, affected by the literal experience of colonialism. Clare Bradford forcefully argues that Nodelman's equation of children and colonialism relegates them to 'a dehistoricized and homogenized category' and sidesteps the idea of race, 'which is central to the binary distinctions between "civilized" and "primitive" on which colonialism and colonial relations were built' (Bradford 2007, 7). Bradford remarks tartly: 'The gently reared middle-class children who comprise the bulk of readers implied by mainstream children's literature are very far removed from the Indigenous peoples who endured the massacres, dispossessions and privations of colonization in Australia, Canada, New Zealand, the Philippines, India, Algeria and many other nations' (Bradford 2011, 274). In the light of the specific experiences of people who have actually experienced colonialism, comparing children as a category to colonialized people is inappropriate and a false equivalency.

In the light of such critiques, postcolonial critics of children's literature tend to focus their inquiries on colonialism in classic and contemporary children's literature, and on the practice of decolonizing children's literature. Alongside their metaphors of childhood as colonized, Nodelman, McGillis, and Kutzer have also enumerated the ways children's literature upheld colonialization, such as the various adventure tales that glorify conquest and the subjection of non-Western nations. Kutzer explains how empire surfaces in British children's texts from the late 19th century well into the post-war period:

> Empire is everywhere in classic children's texts of the late nineteenth century, and its presence continues well into the twentieth. It appears as major setting and, arguably, as character in Kipling's fiction; functions as *deus es machina* in the works of Burnett and Nesbit; raises troubling questions for Lofting; invades children's play in the works of Milne and Ransome; and can even be found between the lines of books published into the 1970s and 1980s, by Susan Cooper and Lynn Reid Banks, among others (Kutzer 2000, xiv).

As we can see from Kutzer's varied list, the workings of empire surface in various ways, including settler colonialism and **imperialism**. Children's texts both of the past and the present 'reinvoke and rehearse colonialism in a variety of ways':

> through narratives that engage with history in realistic or fantastic modes; through sequences involving encounters between Indigenous and non-Indigenous characters; through representations of characters of mixed ancestry; and through metaphorical and symbolic treatments of colonization (Bradford 2007, 3).

We might think of pioneer narratives, where white settlers are depicted as 'heroic, resourceful, godfearing, and intelligent' and Indigenous people seen as 'cowardly, indolent, savage, and stupid' (Bradford 1997, 93). Even fanciful, light-hearted books might have a colonialist underpinning, as we see from the presence of the enslaved, or perhaps indentured, Oompa-Loompas in Roald Dahl's *Charlie and the Chocolate Factory* (1964). Sendak's *Where the Wild Things Are* (1963) is a case in point. Michael Scott Joseph asserts that 'Max's heroic subjugation of the intimidating but then gratefully subservient Wild Things is a reenactment *par excellence* of the colonialist ideal of imposing order upon the other' (Joseph 1997, 160). Max's journey, rather than a child's assertion of independence, can be read as a gleeful enactment of imperialism.

Efforts to decolonize involve the production of books that move beyond the political and social assumptions of empire, including works in Indigenous languages. As one example of many, we might consider India's Children's Book Trust: 'After Indian independence in 1947, the trust was set up to provide books for Indian children in some of the many languages used in this huge country' (Cave and Ayad 2017, 35). Bradford explains that Indigenous publishing houses saw the urgency of providing children 'with reading material which proceeds from Indigenous cultures and which treats as normal and usual the values and practices of these cultures' (Bradford 2011, 274). Indigenous texts, she affirms, must be read within the assumptions of their cultures, rather than within Western frameworks. Noting Canadian books such as Shyam Selvadurai's *Funny Boy* (1994), set in Sri Lanka, and Althea Trotman's *How the East Pond Got its Flowers* (1991), a picture-book about slavery in Antigua, Roderick McGillis and Meena Khorana note: 'we can introduce our children to works of literature that represent the range of cultural experiences and histories that make up the national and international communities that touch all of us' (McGillis and Khorana 1997, 10). These efforts do seem like a useful means of making an imaginative leap into a more global perspective, although the process of engaging with the global in a genuine rather than superficial way is the work of prolonged study and reflection.

A postcolonial approach to children's literature involves challenging the notion of a 'universal,' Eurocentric human character, similar to what we saw in our consideration of race and children's literature. Nigerian writer Chinua Achebe recounts how he once thought European children's books would help his child's development, only to discover their colonialist content: 'Our complacency was well and truly rebuked by the poison we now saw wrapped and taken home to our little girl. I learned that if I wanted a safe book for my child I should at least read it through and at best write it myself' (Achebe 2009, 71). The remedy seems straightforward, but as the turbulent events of Achebe's own novel, *Things Fall Apart* (1958), indicate, separating the writer from a colonial past and education is not quite as easy in practice, notwithstanding the desire to decolonize.

Writing about Australian postcolonial children's books, Bradford notes that they are 'products not of a brave new world "post" colonialization, but of social, cultural, and political realities grounded in colonialization' (Bradford 1997, 90). There is therefore a 'continued need for a postcolonial studies that remains attentive to the effects and legacies of colonialism and, in many cases, continued colonialism' (Snell 2017, 177). Postcolonial theory offers a vision of a children's literature where texts by Indigenous and non-Indigenous producers offer 'diverse, self-conscious, and informed representations of Indigenous cultures' (Bradford 2007, 227), and that reckon honestly and fully with the legacies, and continued presence, of colonialization.

Ecocriticism

Another field that seeks to re-make human relationships with the world on a global scale is ecocriticism. Carolyn Sigler traces the emergence of ecocriticism as an interdisciplinary field in the last 20 years

> in response to growing academic concern about the responses of literature and literary theory to the global crisis of environmental degradation. Both ethically and practically, ecocriticism decenters humanity's importance in nonhuman nature and nature writing (thus rejecting anthropocentric views) and instead explores the complex interrelationships between the human and the nonhuman (a biocentric view) (Sigler 1994, 148).

Cheryll Glotfelty defines ecocriticism quite broadly as the 'study of the relationship between literature and the physical environment,' with the potential for an 'earth-centered approach to literary studies' (Glotfelty 1996, xviii). Dobrin and Kidd refer to the 'mutual history of children's literature and environmental writing and activism' (Dobrin and Kidd 2004, 3), noting that 'classic children's literature has long been preoccupied with natural history, ecology, and human-animal interaction' (Dobrin and Kidd 2004, 4). Sometimes, as in Victorian and Edwardian fantasies such as Charles Kingsley's *The Water Babies* (1863) or Kenneth Grahame's *The Wind in the Willows* (1908), nature was transformed into 'little more than a safe and untroubled embodiment of escape from the corrupt world of civilization' (Sigler 1994, 150). Later, early 20th century children's literature began to include 'a pastoral tradition that includes wild nature' (Sigler 1994: 150), with Gene-Stratton Porter's *A Girl of the Limberlost* (1909) anticipating this movement (Sigler 1994, 150).

Ecocritical approaches attend to the many urban spaces of children's literature as well as rural and **pastoral** settings, considering the complex interactions between natural environments and built spaces. For example, Jenny Bavidge focuses on how New York City children's narratives often feature 'children making or finding very small areas of garden or green, from window boxes to rooftop "beaches"' (Bavidge 2014, 60). In Faith Ringgold's *Tar Beach* (1991) the protagonist, Cassie, leaves her rooftop beach to fly over the city streets, which is described by Bavidge as 'enchanting the city' (Bavidge 2014, 60). Ecocritics read the city as 'a place of complex and interrelated ecologies, networks, and relations' (Bavidge 2014, 69). It is notable that these green spaces are not the nostalgic green places of pastoral children's literature; rather, organic life emerges from within the gritty spaces of the urban built environment.

Environmental crisis and the urgency of teaching a new generation an ethic of preserving—indeed saving—the earth is a motivating force for much ecocriticism in the field of children's literature. Whether these lessons are genuinely effective, or reaching their young audiences with sufficient force, is another question. Clare Echterling, for example, has lamented the ways in which environmental children's texts often 'resign environmental action almost completely to individual choices and behaviors and disassociate environmental crises from their larger constitutive contexts,' such as class disparities and other socio-political concerns (Echterling 2016a, 297). She therefore argues for an ecocriticism informed by insights from postcolonialism. Considering books from the 'golden age' of British literature, for example, Echterling notes their publication at the 'height of British imperialism, massive global environmental change, and the formation of imperial conservation practices and environmental ideas that are still very much with us today' (Echterling 2016b, 93). In her postcolonial ecocritical reading of C.S. Lewis's *The Chronicles of Narnia* she poses questions which ecocritics might be well advised to take as their starting points.

> Do imperial ideas about nature permeate this text? If so, how? What kinds of environmentalism, environmental stewardship, and/or conservation practices does the text promote? To what extent and in what ways is the environmentality of the text intertwined with imperial knowledge and values? Who is presented as a just and legitimate environmental steward? Conversely, who commits crimes against nature? In other words, who are the 'eco-villains?' Are particular groups of people aligned with nonhuman nature or depicted as being less-than-human? What types of places or environments are portrayed as valuable and worthy of esteem and preservation? Which are depicted as evil, dangerous, invaluable, or valuable only in economic terms? Finally, does the text present historically and culturally specific ideas about nature as universal? (Echterling 2016b, 97–98).

These questions offer a holistic approach to the consideration of nonhuman nature.

Involved in this new awareness is an understanding that the formative ecocritical texts of the past may not meet all of the needs of the present or speak to every region. Dr. Seuss's *The Lorax* (1971), a work critical of the exploitation of natural resources, is a good example. A young boy encounters the remorseful Once-ler, who tells him the story of how he decimated the natural environment by overproducing garments called 'Thneeds,' made from the all-important Truffala Trees. The Lorax of the title is an animated, passionate figure who emerges from the trunk of the first tree felled by the Once-ler, to declare 'I am the Lorax. I speak for the trees' (Seuss 1971, n.p.). The ending of the book is often interpreted as a call to action for its young readers. The book's young auditor is given the last remaining Truffala Tree seed and told: 'UNLESS someone like you cares a whole awful lot, nothing is going to get better. It's not.' (Seuss 1971, n.p.).

Due in large part to its sinuous, inventive, and playful language and its fantastic visual depiction of a world of Truffala Trees, Humming-Fish, Bar-ba-loots and Swomee-Swans, *The Lorax* has become the 'go to' book in ecocritical children's literature. Many critics continue to sing its praises, as Eliza Darling does when she marvels over 'Seuss's uncanny faculty for capturing 500 years of industrialization, urbanization and environmental degradation in a few capricious pages' and 'his ability to describe the inherent contradictions of the capitalist mode of production which eventually lead to its own collapse' (Darling 2001, 53). In inventing the multi-purpose Thneed, Seuss captures the ability of capitalism to invent and stimulate new consumer needs. Matthew Teorey argues that the book calls for a salutary balance of 'economic development and healthy, diverse ecosystems. It is the vehicles with multiple axes and the Once-ler's over-harvesting and refusal to replant that are the problem' (Teorey 2014, 335).

While the book is clearly appreciated, there is an increasing sense that the political models espoused by the Lorax are not necessarily efficacious: 'The Lorax was a polemic about pollution, impassioned and bristling with confrontation and name-calling' (Morgan and Morgan 1995, 211). As an advocate for the trees, the Lorax is relentless and hectoring. He shouts down his opponents, in a voice 'sharpish and bossy' (Seuss 1971, n.p). The Lorax's rhetorical choices are not just hostile but could be seen as counterproductive, undermining his own goal of speaking for the trees: 'The Lorax does not attempt to appeal to the Once-ler in terms that he might understand. For example, he makes no attempt to argue for careful and considered use of natural resources on the grounds of ESD (Economically Sustainable Development)' (Pleasants 2006, 184).

Instead of retaining *The Lorax* as the pre-eminent text for environmental education, Kathleen Pleasants argues, we should gravitate towards environmental literature that is more responsive to local environmental contexts, in her case Australia. Certainly, *The Lorax* does reflect Seuss's own particular preoccupations and concerns. Although he completed the book in Kenya, Seuss first got the idea when looking out at his view of the north coast of San Diego, 'shores that had been empty when he first came and now teemed with condominiums and look-alike houses' (Morgan and Morgan 1995, 209). His own blissful enclave was foremost in his mind. Indeed, the Edenic world before the Once-ler arrives depicts an unrealistic natural world without predators and prey: a pristine 'original state' reminiscent of Romantic-era idealizations of nature (Darling 2001, 54; Pleasants 2006, 185). *The Lorax* is a great achievement in myth-making but Pleasants' critique rings true, and the book benefits from being placed in conversation with books with a different approach to environmental conservation, or ones that are more attentive to cultural nuances. It should certainly be supplemented with a range of other ecological visions in children's literature.

Both ecocriticism and postcolonial theory look at children's literature to ask who holds power and how that power is used. They consider what children's literature can tell us about damage to the earth and to people, and also offer sustainable models of living in harmony with nature if human beings are to flourish. Children's literature is capable of registering the environmental and political injustices of the past, often exploring other ways of approaching the earth and human relationships all over the world.

Animal studies and posthumanism

Karin Lesnik-Oberstein estimates that 'on average, at least two-thirds of the books [in children's bookstores] are in some form or another linked with nature and the environment, and—specifically and most importantly—with animals' (Lesnik-Oberstein 1998, 208). Why are animal stories viewed as so suitable for children and what is their cultural function in children's literature? Animal stories have, of course, long been used as a vehicle to instruct children about social and political life, especially in fables, where, as we have already seen, 'the animals are not really themselves, but disguised people' (Blount 1975, 15). We see this both in ancient texts like Aesop's and in more recent books, such as Roald Dahl's *Fabulous Mr. Fox* (1970) or Doreen Cronin's *click clack moo: cows that type* (2000), which is a fable for the power of a union's collective bargaining. George Orwell's *Animal Farm* (1945), where two pigs, Snowball and Napoleon, lead a successful revolt against a farmer, with Napoleon later emerging as a totalitarian leader, was intended as an allegory of the failed ideals of the Russian Revolution.

Anthropomorphism—the attributing of human traits to animals—has 'humanized' the animal world in children's literature. T.S. Eliot's *Old Possum's Book of Practical Cats* (1939) is a book of whimsical poems about feline psychology and the pursuits of several singular cats like the frail but venerated theatre cat Gus to Mr Mistoffelees, who, in the guise of a hunt for mice, is devoted to magic and sleights of hand. While these characters emerge as supremely cat-like, they are also very much human in their interests and personalities: theatre, or magic, or criminal activity. Despite their human preoccupations and qualities, Eliot's cats are not merely stand-ins for people, or symbols for humans. Eliot, Stacy Rule argues, has used the unique capacities of poetry to facilitate a cross-species engagement by offering 'advice about how readers might approach autonomous and internally complex animals and imagines how they might address us' (Rule 2011, 155). We see this, for example, in Eliot's poems 'The Naming of Cats,' where cats are described as possessing their own secret names which no human knows, and 'The Addressing of Cats,' which gently lays down protocols for approaching a cat; finally reaching the goal of calling a cat by his name, with the understanding that a cat is *not* a dog. This ultimately leads to 'an equalization of the two species [human and cat] based on singular personalities' (Rule 2011, 156). Eliot's poetry helps us see these singular cats as having agency and interests in their own right and not just as reflections of human concerns, as in the case of 'Skimbleshanks: the Railway Cat,' where the rhythms of the poetry reflect the cat's preoccupation. *Old Possum's Book of Practical Cats* also stages a tension between order and disorder in keeping with the concerns of Eliot's modernist period. We see, for example, cats who keep things in line, such as Skimbleshanks, who watches over the Night Mail train ('You can play no pranks with Skimbleshanks!'), or the diligent mouser Jennyanydots, and those like

Macavity ('who could defy the law') who serve to disrupt order. Because it is comic verse with inventive rhymes, its poetic form might be assumed to be simple. But the variations of rhythm in the poetic form make its anthropomorphism more complicated, with irregular line lengths not arranged in a conventional stanza form. Rule argues that *Old Possum's Book of Practical Cats* challenges two assumptions: 'children's poetry is unsophisticated, and animals are simple beings' (Rule 2011, 150).

Another example of a text that uses anthropomorphism to reflect human concerns but which can be read as carving out a space for animal subjectivity is Kenneth Grahame's *The Wind in the Willows* (1908). Mole, Rat, Badger, and Toad, the anthropomorphic River Bank dwellers, display a very human class prejudice against the weasels and stoats of the Wild Wood. Yet Catherine Elick sees *The Wind in the Willows* as genuinely capturing animal **ontologies**, or ways of being: 'What has usually been interpreted as a class conflict between the River-Bank animals and the Wild-Wood creatures can also be interpreted as a battle to define true animal nature and determine how animals should live' (Elick 2015, 50). A segment devoted to the god Pan 'also represents an attempt at constructing a religion for and of animals' (Cosslett 2006, 7). Elick's and Tess Cosslett's readings represent an interesting departure from the critical consensus that these works merely reflect human ways of living, contending instead that *The Wind in the Willows* gives animals emotions, thought, and religion separate from human beings.

Sometimes the use of animal figures to signify human social structures can be a source of irritation for critics, who see it as a distorted portrayal of animal behaviour. Richard Adams cites R. M. Lockley's *Private Life of the Rabbit* as a source for *Watership Down* (1972), but LeGuin notes that Adams's world is 'a militaristic patriarchy in which males do all planning, thinking, and acting,' passing it off as animal behaviour when Lockley had made it clear that female rabbits were the leaders in nature (LeGuin 2004, 26). A successful animal story does not require an accurate portrayal of animal life as found in nature, but Adams stated that he sought to portray rabbits scientifically, and so LeGuin's remarks ring true. At the same time, *Watership Down* is undeniably perspicacious about the difficulties faced by animals when humans destroy their habitat, speaking to the animal's position in the face of human domination.

One cultural function of animal stories is to make children aware of how much animals can and do suffer. Animal autobiographies, fictionalized first-person accounts of an animal's life, are one cultural location for this kind of empathy. They flourished in England and North America after 1824, following the founding of the first animal welfare organization: the Society for the Prevention of Cruelty to Animals. In this genre, 'animals speak with excruciating candor about their suffering at the hands of humans' (Elick 2015, 8). The most famous example, *Black Beauty* (1877), about a wronged cab-horse, helped bring about a ban on the equine bearing rein or checkrein, a fashionable rein that forced horses to hold up their heads uncomfortably high (Elick 2015, 8; Cosslett 2006, 74).

Animal autobiographies form part of an 'education in sympathy' (Cosslett 2006, 63), but they spark several questions:

> How is animal subjectivity created, and how is this subjectivity linked to the books' ethical purposes? ... How is the issue of animal language dealt with? How is the actual scene of writing or narration imagined? Who is the narratee or implied audience for these stories? Do animal narrators have a different kind of consciousness to the human, and/or are they built up with analogies with human types? (Cosslett 2006, 65).

Questions that seem purely formal—such as 'how can an animal write its own autobiography?'—underscore the form's artificiality, but also the author's desire to represent an otherwise ignored or disrespected subjectivity. At the same time it is clear that the subjectivity is very much one which is constructed by the author and imposed upon the animal character. There is also a sense that, no matter how many reversals of power the text encodes, humans remain very much in charge. We might think of all those works where children are encouraged to be humane, but even that humanity is an extension of their power. Amy Ratelle considers how children's literature and film encourage identification with animals, both implicitly and explicitly, but then require children 'to position themselves as distinctly human through the mode of their interactions with both lived animals and those depicted in literature and film' (Ratelle 2015, 10). A child may be encouraged to be more humane, without renouncing the power that they hold over animals. A motif where children change places with animals is one 'rhetorical device of reversing roles, translating animal pain into the equivalent human pain' (Cosslett 2006, 14). In P.L. Travers' *Mary Poppins* (1934), for example, 'the children pay a visit to the Zoo after dark and find animals in charge and humans caged' (Cosslett 2006, 59).

Can human beings really imagine the lives of animals apart from their involvement in human life? Writers have tried. Sara Pennypacker's *Pax* (2016), illustrated by Jon Klassen, is the tale of a young boy, Peter, whose father shames him into abandoning his beloved pet fox, Pax. Realizing his mistake, the boy journeys into the wilderness to bring Pax home; the chapters alternate between the point of view of the boy and that of the fox. Pax grieves his separation from the boy but comes to understand his own wild nature. At the end of the novel the boy finds Pax, only to realize that he must be left in the wild, where he now belongs. *Pax* is perhaps an extension of the tradition of wilderness tales like Ernest Thompson Seton's *Wild Animals I Have Known* (1898), set within the Canadian wilderness and espousing an ethic of conservation. But *Pax* is also a contemporary attempt to depict human renunciation of control over animal lives, and an acknowledgement that their lives and destinies might be, and should be, entirely separate from our own.

Animal studies' approaches sometimes include a consideration of what is termed 'the **posthuman**,' which describes an entity or person who exists beyond the state of being a human, or a person who is comprised of human and machine. Elaine Ostry argues that the posthuman emerges when the lines between 'organic and inorganic' and 'human and animal' are crossed through technology or other forms of cultural change: 'What it means to be human has never been more flexible, manipulated, or in question' (Ostry 2004, 222). In the wake of these changing definitions of 'the human,' children's literature tests and plays with the boundaries between human and animal, human and vegetable, and human and machine.

One contemporary cultural space where we see, in Holly Batty's words, 'a reconsideration of the human/animal binary' is the *Harry Potter* series (Batty 2015, 26). Harry morphs into a being with gills in the Triwizard tournament, animagi transform from people into animals, and Sirius Black engages with the animal side of his nature as a werewolf within wizard society. Harry Potter has an affinity for snakes and speaks Parseltongue; in *The Order of the Phoenix* he has a dream from a snake's point of view (Batty 2015, 35). In this reading of posthumanism in *Harry Potter,* Harry has not just blurred the boundaries between human and animal, but become himself something other than human, or more than human.

Posthumanist approaches also focus on the permeable boundaries between child and machine. Zoe Jaques affirms that 'childhood has slipped indelibly towards the posthuman. The growth of TV and computer ownership places machine-mediated fantasy before the eyes of children as a part of daily life' (Jaques 2015a, 5). Robots and toys in children's literature, such as those seen in Pixar/Disney's *WALL-E* and *Toy Story* films, 'give child readers alternative ways of imagining human interconnections with the artificial' (Jaques, 2015b, 20). Theories of the posthuman make us suddenly aware of the many inanimate objects that quicken into life in children's literature, such as Carlo Collodi's *Pinocchio* (1883) or the Tin Woodman of Oz whose 'meat body' is slowly replaced by animate tin (although his old-fashioned yen for a heart marks him as a quintessential liberal humanist). Posthumanist children's literature, like animal studies, necessitates a playful engagement with the biological limits of humanity, and an acknowledgement of the ways in which posthumanism challenges our existing models of identity and subjectivity. It is that playful engagement that marks my case study of *Flora and Ulysses*, a book that depicts powerful human-animal relationships and the rediscovery of human connection in a new mode.

Case study: Flora and Ulysses

Flora Belle Buckman, the protagonist of Kate DiCamillo's Newbery Award-winning *Flora and Ulysses: The Illuminated Adventures* (2013), is a 'natural-born cynic' (DiCamillo 2013, 6) still reeling from her parents' recent divorce. She is devoted to the comic book adventures of THE AMAZING INCANDESTO, although her mother makes her sign a contract pledging to 'work to turn her face away from the idiotic high jinks of comics and toward the bright light of true literature' (DiCamillo 2013, 5). *Flora and Ulysses* pays tribute to popular culture as empowering for child readers; some of the action of the book is related through comic book panels rather than through conventional text.

Flora's life changes irreversibly when a hapless squirrel is sucked up into a runaway vacuum—the Ulysses 2000X—in her backyard. The squirrel acquires human consciousness and a flair for writing poetry on a typewriter. Flora's neighbour names him Ulysses, after the offending (yet transformative) vacuum. Flora's mother, who is no friend to poetry-writing squirrels, enlists her ex-husband to kill Ulysses. Ulysses's escape and deepening bond with Flora leads to a transformation in human, as well as human-animal, relationships when Flora's father helps her save Ulysses. By the end of the novel, Flora and her mother also experience a long-needed *rapprochement,* and, indeed, Roberta Seelinger Trites reads the novel within feminist thought on the 'ethics of care' and relationality (Trites 2018, 178–179). Questions of childhood **agency**, such as those foregrounded by Childhood Studies, are also relevant, with Flora joining the many child protagonists who must defy adults. Animal studies might help us to understand the strong bond that develops between Flora and Ulysses, whether it is a cultural distortion of his animal nature, and the implications of a squirrel developing anthropomorphizing traits such as the capacity for writing poetry.

One of the novel's signature attributes, in fact, is its insistence on a squirrel's point of view, which can be seen as a human projection onto the animal world. One theme is Ulysses's insistent greed and desire for food; he ends one of his poems with the heartfelt line 'I am very, very hungry' (DiCamillo 2013, 65). Like many animal protagonists in children's literature, Ulysses has endured violence in the past: 'It was a sad fact of his existence as a squirrel that there was always someone, somewhere, who wanted him dead' (DiCamillo 2013, 76). Yet Ulysses experiences a revelation after his encounter with the vacuum. One of the most affecting scenes in the novel is when he is moved—'his eyes bright'—by a neighbour's reading of a Rilke poem (DiCamillo 2013, 82). In children's literature, relationships with animals often precipitate a change in perspective, and this novel also provides a squirrel with new perceptions and capacities.

Flora's mother is distressed by what she perceives as Flora's 'strangeness.' Her mother writes romance novels with titles like *On Feathered Wings of Joy* and simply cannot understand Flora's devotion to comic books. Flora is illustrated as wearing large glasses and sporting a severe haircut, traits that do not conform to traditional notions of femininity. Her foil and antagonist is a very feminine china shepherdess lamp, with fluffy skirt and pink cheeks, owned and adored by her mother and suspected by Flora to be more like the daughter she would prefer. Flora's deep attachment to a squirrel strikes her mother as disturbingly unconventional:

> Flora Belle. She is a strange child. And the world is not kind to the strange. She was strange before, and she's stranger now. Now she is walking around with a squirrel on her shoulder. Talking to a squirrel. Talking to a typing, flying squirrel. Not good. Not good at all.
> ...
> I want a daughter who is happy. I want her to have friends who aren't squirrels. I don't want her to end up unloved and all alone in the world (DiCamillo 2013, 195–196).

Flora's mother wants to constrain her daughter within her vision of a safe and acceptable life, yet the novel also shows an adult whose thinking becomes more flexible and who subsequently rearranges her own priorities. Late in the novel her mother's beloved china shepherdess is broken in an altercation with a violent cat. Rather than mourn the shepherdess, as Flora assumed she would, Flora's mother focuses instead on her daughter:

> Her mother stepped over the pieces of the broken little shepherdess.
> She took Flora into her arms.
> 'My baby,' said her mother.
> 'Me?' said Flora.
> 'You,' said her mother (DiCamillo 2013, 225).

Flora realizes that she is her mother's beloved child after all and, in the words of Trites, 'finds strength in allowing herself to be both the one-caring and the cared-for—and to become in her process of growing more relational' (Trites 2018: 175).

One relationship that Flora builds is with William Spiver, the boy next door, who consistently annoys her but who she comes to trust as she tries to save Ulysses. The bond between Flora and Spiver seems rather chaste, a matter of some handholding, pointing to friendship rather than *eros*, but her trust in him mimics the interdependence of conjugality. Like most children's books, the portrayal of sexuality, if that is what it can be called, is rather oblique here. It is interesting to note that Flora does not renounce her relationship with Ulysses in favour of her friendship with Spiver, as Fern Arable does in *Charlotte's Web* when she leaves Wilbur to ride the Ferris wheel with Henry Fussy. The friendship is not treated as part of a developmental trajectory of giving up childhood attachments, as we see in so many of the narratives considered by Eric L. Tribunella, where a boy must wrenchingly renounce a dog in order to reach a painful maturation.

Spiver is a puzzling character in some ways, although disability theory might help us understand him better. At the beginning of the book he believes himself to have been blinded by a traumatic event related to family tensions and a quarrel with his mother and stepfather. He wears dark glasses and has trouble navigating his environment, but his Great-Aunt Tootie Tickham tells him, bluntly, that he is not blind. We might read Spiver's belief in his blindness as an example of the 'narrative prosthesis' articulated by Mitchell and Snyder: a mere plot device. Trites certainly see it as a 'metaphor for another type of cloaking or veiling; he cannot allow himself to see the truth that he is the person who has damaged his own relationship with his mother (by pushing his stepfather's truck into a pond)' (Trites 2018, 178). Yet his belief in his own blindness might also be read as disabling in its own right; while convinced that he is blind he finds it hard to get around. When Spiver's glasses are knocked off, he realizes that he has never been blind. This might be the novel's way of making fun of the 'miracle cures' of classic children's literature, but some disability studies approaches might object to DiCamillo's use of blindness as a metaphor, or to the critical consideration of blindness in purely metaphorical terms.

Flora and Ulysses has much to tell us about child agency. To save Ulysses, Flora has to assert her own authority when her mother proves hostile to her squirrel, sneaking out of the home at night and seeking alliances with adults such as Great-Aunt Tootie and Dr Meescham, an eccentric woman living in her father's building. *Flora and Ulysses* is so rewarding to consider in the light of new theories and methodologies of children's literature criticism because it charts a wide range of affective possibilities for child readers, across the species, across generations, and across different gender expressions. *Flora and Ulysses* thus has elements in common with Cece Bell's *El Deafo* that we considered earlier, including a difficult journey from isolation to connection, the use of imagined super-heroes as a means of expressing agency (in Flora's case her squirrel Ulysses holds those powers), and the key role played by friendship. While some critics are unconvinced that children's literature can foster empathy in its readers, *Flora and Ulysses* repeatedly explores dramatic changes of perspective, from a squirrel who becomes a skilled poet to a girl who learns that she is valued and in turn can better value the people around her.

CONCLUSION

As a phenomenon, children's literature is in many ways paradoxical. It is meant to initiate novice readers into the 'ways of the world' but often expected to preserve childhood innocence in the process. Children's literature immerses children in the normative ethos of the dominant culture, yet can also function as a space to nurture transformative social change and to cultivate young people's rebellious instincts. It appears to encourage individuals to develop as autonomous subjects in pursuit of their individual interests but also explores relational selfhoods and community. These contradictions and others make it difficult to generalize about the nature and cultural function of children's literature. In fact, scholars of Children's Literature frequently do their best work when they focus their attention on works and literary movements that challenge our preconceptions of what children's literature is and what it should be. We might think, for example, of work that finds 'knowing' rather than 'innocent' children in historical children's literature, such as the sophisticated 'artful dodgers' described by Marah Gubar in Victorian children's culture. There are also the many literary works for children where childhood innocence is not a desired quality, as we see from Ann González's work on the savvy, adept 'trickster figures' of Central American and Caribbean children's literature. We can also see, in work by Robin Bernstein and others, how childhood innocence has functioned for a long time as a privilege denied to children of colour.

Children's literature has always responded to the perceived cultural and social needs of young people: from the medieval **courtesy books** that taught the etiquette needed for the social harmony of extended family households to contemporary works that tackle the complex social dynamics of our time. In any given period of literary history, however, children's literature can offer sharply contrasting messages. For example, 19th century children's literature produced the whimsical nonsense of writers such as Edward Lear and Lewis Carroll, encouraging anarchic play, but also offered many narratives of social conformity and personal restraint through the didactic texts that flourished in the period. Perhaps children of the period were thought to need both whimsy and discipline at different times. Alternatively, we might see the history of children's literature as marked by a contest between warring visions of children's literature and the qualities it should embody.

In many ways, children's literature continues to exist because adults are determined to carve out a distinct literary and cultural space for young people in the face of profound cultural and technological change. But the adaptation of these works in multiple fields and the success of 'cross-over' works like the *Harry Potter* series may be a sign that children's literature—as well as the film, television, and game adaptations of works for children—hearkens back to one of its earliest moments as shared adult-child culture rather than a cultural enclave for young people alone. This is another contradiction of children's literature: a literature that exists for the needs of younger people may ultimately belong to all readers equally, while still existing as a literary market that is tailored to younger people.

As it always has done, children's literature registers cultural change and to some extent drives it. Through moments of insight into the natural world and animal life we can catch a glimpse in children's literature of new ways of being human, and in the process rethink human society. There is a renewed sense of urgency to educate children about the new world they will face in the 21st century. We see new attention to questions of stewardship of the earth and a truer reckoning with historical atrocities. As an academic field, Children's Literature is fully established across multiple disciplines and is constantly renewed by new methodologies and cultural concerns. New developments include a stronger sense in English departments of what other disciplines can teach us, and attempts to break down the division between 'book people' and 'child people.' We are also gleaning new insights from current research into cognition and children's attainment of literacy. Global histories and histories of little-known literary movements promise to productively unsettle the established contours of the field. The loop between activists, writers, and scholars has encouraged diversity and pressed for the inclusion of marginalized voices, and this changes our sense of a universal childhood and a literature responding to that childhood. The scholar who works in Children's Literature must now—more than ever—see the works they study within these wider cultural concerns, with the study of children's books all the more urgent and rewarding for that fact.

GLOSSARY

Ableism	The assumption that a non-disabled body is superior to a disabled one, and that a disability requires a 'cure.'
Absurdism	A literary genre where characters cannot find any innate meaning or purpose in life, calling into question concepts like truth or value.
Affect theory	The analysis of 'affects,' which is a term sometimes used interchangeably with 'emotions.' Affect theory considers how these 'affects' are experienced subjectively and within political and social life.
Age levelling	The sorting of books into age-appropriate categories like 'Ages 5–9' or grade levels like 'Middle Grade.'
Agency	Control that children have over their own navigation of culture despite their relative powerlessness in political and social life.
Alterity	'Otherness,' or the state of being different.
Animal studies	An emerging branch of scholarship that seeks to investigate the relationship between people

and non-human animals, and the cultural representation and shaping of those relationships.

Anthropomorphism The attribution of human traits to animals.

Avant-garde Experimental ideas and methods in arts and literature.

Battledores A reading technology that superseded the hornbook. Battledores were made from cardboard with a paper overlay over a paddle shape; they dropped out of production in the 19th century.

Blending A theory of cognition developed by Mark Turner and Gilles Fauconnier to describe how the brain combines different ideas, words, and images to make new meanings from these combinations in a network of 'mental spaces.'

Carnivalesque Mikhail Bakhtin's term for a literary mode that challenges dominant power structures and celebrates subversive misrule through chaos and humour.

Chapbooks Inexpensive booklets written in a wide variety of genres, including tales of adventure, folk, and fairy tales, often regarded as one of the first iterations of popular culture.

Childhood Studies An interdisciplinary field that studies the experience of childhood historically and in the present, as well as questions of child agency and children's rights.

Childness Peter Hollindale's term for the qualities that a child brings to children's literature, and the qualities that mark a work of children's literature as being for children.

Childist Peter Hunt's term for reading as far as possible from a child's point of view. John Wall uses 'childism' to mean that our ethical life should be completely transformed by attending to children's needs and perspectives.

Cisgender Identifying with the biological sex of one's birth.

Cognitive narratology	An interdisciplinary study drawing on the disciplines of biology, neuroscience, and psychology, as well as child development that considers the cognitive capacities that young people bring to their readings of texts, as shaped both by biology and culture.
Colonialism	The process by which a country attains control over another country, settling it and exploiting it culturally and/or economically.
Concept picture-books	Picture-books that teach children the alphabet, their numbers, and so on.
Courtesy literature	Books dealing with etiquette, manners, and behaviour; part of the didactic literature of the medieval period.
Decolonization	The undoing of colonialism, usually by a nation seeking independence and autonomy, but also all cultural practices that seek to oppose colonial domination.
Dialogism	Mikhail Bakhtin's idea that a work has a multiplicity of perspectives and voices, as seen in the novel form, and where each work is informed by and responds to other works. See also **heteroglossia.**
Discourse	The sum of social ideas and practices, including language and cultural representation.
Ecocriticism	The study of literature's relationship with physical environments, particularly the natural world.
Embourgeoisement	Inculcation of middle-class ideals.
Empathy	Insight into another person's thoughts and feelings, and sharing in those feelings.
Eurocentrism	A bias towards Western or European civilization, and the centring of Europe in scholarship and education.
Evangelical movement	Religious revival of the early 19th century that resulted in a number of religious works for children distributed by the Society for the

Promotion of Christian Knowledge and the Religious Tract Society.

Fables A story, usually with animals, conveying a moral.

Fan fiction Fiction written by a fan of a particular book, television series, movie, etc. that draws on the characters and/or setting of the original work. It is rarely authorized by the author or producer of the original work.

Gender-fluid people Gender-fluid people do not identify with any fixed gender identity.

Golden age The period where many of the books acknowledged as children's literary classics today were published (1865–1915).

Heteroglossia Mikhail Bakhtin's term for the 'many voices' that a text can contain, with a plurality of voices creating a polyphonic work.

Heteronormativity The presumption that heterosexual relations are the norm.

Hornbook A primer for study used from the 15th to the 18th centuries, where a sheet of paper with the letters of the alphabet or a religious text was mounted on a wooden frame with a protective sheet of transparent horn (or bone). The hornbook often had a hole punched in its handle so it could hang from a child's belt or girdle.

Ideology The normative practices of a society or group, often working on an unconscious level to shape individual subjectivities.

Ideological state apparatus Louis Althusser's term for social, cultural, and state structures—organized religion, law, education, and the family—that convey the state's values through cultural means, unlike the direct violence of prisons, the military, and the police (repressive state apparatus).

Imperialism Use of colonization, military force, or other means to exert power over another nation or group.

Indigenous people	People who inhabited a country or geographic region before the conquest or colonization of that country or region, and the people descended from them.
Interdisciplinary	Involving or drawing on more than one branch of knowledge; combining the insights of more than one discipline.
Intersectional feminism	A feminist practice that acknowledges that oppression is shaped by race, class, disability, and sexuality rather than just gender; the term was coined by legal scholar Kimberlé Crenshaw.
Kinship model	Marah Gubar's model of children's literature where children are seen as part of a 'family' of readers, in a network of relationships.
Modernism	A literary movement of the late 19th and early 20th centuries in prose and poetry that sought to break with traditional literary forms.
Narrative prosthesis	David T. Mitchell and Sharon L. Snyder's term for the ways in which disability has been used as a narrative trope, with narratives depending on disability for their literary effects
Neurodiversity	The many different ways in which cognition and perception are experienced by individuals, including conditions such as autism, ADHD, dyslexia, and others.
Niche publications	Published books for a highly specialized market.
Non-binary people	Non-binary people do not identify as either a man or a woman, either because they identify as a man or woman at different times, consider themselves to be in-between the categories of man and woman, or define their gender as outside these categories altogether.
Ontologies	Pertaining to the nature of being and ways of being.

Orientalism	Exoticized fantasies held about Arab and Asian people that western scholars and travellers used to justify colonial ventures.
Pastoral	Portraying an idealized version of life in the country.
Performative	A form of utterance that effects change through the process of being spoken or written.
Postcolonial literature	The literary productions of a country after colonial rule, with attention to the legacy of colonialism and imperialism and the continued presence of colonizing forces.
Posthuman	An entity or person who exists beyond the state of being a human, or a person who is comprised of human and machine or human and non-human animal.
Propaganda	A work that contains clearly biased information specifically and consciously intended to promote a point of view or political position.
Puritans	An amorphous religious group that refused to conform to the requirements of the national religion as practised by the Church of England, feeling that its organization and forms of worship needed both reform and simplification.
Rational moralists	A group of writers in the 18th century who stressed the power of didactic children's literature to cultivate young people's reason.
Repressive state apparatus	Louis Althusser's term for the arms of state power that proceed via violence, such as prisons, the army, the police, and so on.
Renaissance humanism	A cultural movement that stressed secular, as opposed to sacred, learning, as well as encouraging a return to Greek and Roman thought.
Romanticism	A movement in arts and literature in the late 18th and early 19th centuries, stressing subjective experience, supernatural or non-rational experiences, and attunement to the natural world.

Schemas	In cognitive narratology, a pattern of thought that helps organize information in patterns.
Scripts	In cognitive narratology, a pattern of thought to help produce a schema for routine activities.
Social model	Theory of disability that argues that the way society is organized is the cause of disability rather than an individual's impairment or difference, with a focus on ways to change social structures to remove barriers for disabled people.
Supercrip	A stereotype where a character with a disability or illness is portrayed as having an extraordinary skill or genius that helps them 'overcome' their disability.
Transgender people	Transgender people identify with a gender identity and/or expression different from the sex they were assigned at birth.
Trickster figures	A mischievous figure in myth or folklore who uses his or her knowledge or skill to disrupt conventions or play tricks, sometimes as a compensation for physical weakness or another disadvantage.

BIBLIOGRAPHY

Abate, Michelle Ann. 2010. *Raising Your Kids Right: Children's Literature and American Political Conservatism*. New Brunswick, NJ: Rutgers University Press.

Abate, Michelle Ann. 2016. *The Big Smallness: Niche Marketing, the American Culture Wars, and the New Children's Literature*. New York: Routledge.

Achebe, Chinua. 2009. *The Education of a British-Protected Child*. New York: Alfred A. Knopf.

Adams, Gillian. 1986. 'The First Children's Literature? The Case for Sumer.' *Children's Literature* 14: 1–30.

Adams, Gillian. 1998. 'Medieval Children's Literature: Its Possibility and Actuality.' *Children's Literature* 26: 1–24.

Aldama, Frederick Luis. 2018. *Latino/a Children's and Young Adult Writers on the Art of Storytelling*. Pittsburgh, PA: University of Pittsburgh Press.

Althusser, Louis. [1968] 1970. *Reading Capital*. London: New Left Books.

Anderson, M.T. 2011. 'Point of Departure.' In *Handbook of Research on Children's Literature*, edited by Shelby A. Wolf, Karen Coats, Patricia Enciso and Christine A. Jenkins, 372–374. New York: Routledge.

Ang, Susan. 2000. *The Widening World of Children's Literature*. New York: St. Martin's Press.

Ariès, Phillipe. 1962. *Centuries of Childhood: A Social History of Family Life*. Translated by Robert Baldick. New York: Vintage Books.

Asim, Jabari. 2014. 'Don't Shy Away From Books About Tough Issues.' *The New York TimesOpinion Pages: Room for Debate*, July 18. https://www.nytimes.com/roomfordebate/2014/07/09/should-books-for-childrens-be-political/dont-shy-away-from-books-about-tough-issues

Bailey, Merridee. 2007. 'In Service and at Home: Didactic Texts for Children and Young People, c. 1400–1600.' *Parergon* 24, no. 2: 23–46.

Balibar, Étienne and Pierre Macherey. [1974] 1981. 'On Literature as an Ideological Form.' In *Untying the Text: A Post-Structuralist Reader*, edited by Robert J. C. Young, 79–99. Boston, MA, and London: Routledge & Kegan Paul.

Baskin, Barbara H. and Karen H. Harris. 1977. *Notes from a Different Drummer: A Guide to Juvenile Fiction Portraying the Handicapped*. New York: R.R. Bowker Company.

Batty, Holly. 2015. 'Harry Potter and the (Post)human Animal Body.' *Bookbird* 53, no. 1: 24–37.

Baum, L. Frank. 1900. *The Wonderful Wizard of Oz*. Illustrated by W. W. Denslow. Chicago, IL: Geo. M. Hill.

Bavidge, Jenny. 2014. '"Cities Will Sing": Natural New York.' In *Children's Literature and New York City*, edited by Pádraic Whyte and Keith O'Sullivan, 57–73. New York: Routledge.

Bayliss, Sarah. 2017. 'How "El Deafo" Empowers Kids Who Are Deaf and Hard of Hearing.' *School Library Journal*, January 31. https://www.slj.com/?detailStory=how-el-deafo-empowers-kids-who-are-deaf-and-hearing-impaired

Beck, Julie. 2014. 'The Adult Lessons of YA Fiction.' *The Atlantic*, June 9. https://www.theatlantic.com/entertainment/archive/2014/06/the-adult-lessons-of-ya-fiction/372417/

Bell, Cece. 2014. *El Deafo*. New York: Amulet Books.

Bernstein, Robin. 2011a. 'Children's Books, Dolls, and the Performance of Race; or, The Possibility of Children's Literature.' *PMLA* 126: 160–169.

Bernstein, Robin. 2011b. *Racial Innocence: Performing American Childhood from Slavery to Civil Rights*. New York: NYU Press.

Bérubé, Michael. 2016. *The Secret Life of Stories: From Don Quixote to Harry Potter, How Understanding Intellectual Disability Transforms the Way We Read*. New York: New York University Press.

Bishop, Rudine Sims. 1990. 'Mirrors, Windows, and Sliding Glass Doors.' *Perspectives: Choosing and Using Books for the Classroom* 6, no. 2: ix–xi.

Blackford, Holly. 2004. *Out of this World: Why Literature Matters to Girls*. New York: Teachers College Press.

Blount, Margaret Joan. 1975. *Animal Land: The Creatures of Children's Fiction*. New York: William Morrow.

Bluebond-Langner, Myra. 1978. *The Private Worlds of Dying Children*. Princeton, NJ: Princeton University Press.

Bradford, Clare. 1997. 'Representing Indigeneity: Aborigines and Australian Children's Literature Then and Now.' *ARIEL: A Review of International English Literature* 28, no. 1: 89–99.

Bradford, Clare. 2001. 'The End of Empire? Colonial and Postcolonial Journeys in Children's Books.' *Children's Literature* 29: 196–218.

Bradford, Clare. 2007. *Unsettling Narratives: Postcolonial Readings of Children's Literature*. Waterloo, Ontario: Wilfrid Laurier University Press.

Bradford, Clare. 2010. 'Race, Ethnicity and Colonialism.' In *The Routledge Companion to Children's Literature*, edited by David Rudd, 39–51. New York: Routledge.

Bradford, Clare. 2011. 'The Case of Children's Literature: Colonial or Anti-Colonial?' *Global Studies of Childhood* 1, no. 4: 271–279.

Bullen, Elizabeth, Kristine Moruzi and Michelle J. Smith. 2018. 'Children's Literature and the Affective Turn.' In *Affect, Emotion, and Children's Literature: Representation and Socialisation in Texts for Children and Young Adults*, edited by Elizabeth Bullen, Kristine Moruzi and Michelle J. Smith, 1–17. New York: Routledge.

Capshaw, Katharine Smith. 2004. *Children's Literature of the Harlem Renaissance*. Bloomington, IN: Indiana University Press.

Capshaw, Katharine Smith. 2011. 'Race.' In *Keywords for Children's Literature*, edited by Philip Nel and Lissa Paul, 189–193. New York: New York University Press.

Capshaw, Katharine Smith. 2014. 'Ethnic Studies and Children's Literature: A Conversation between Fields.' *The Lion and the Unicorn* 38, no. 3: 237–257.

Capshaw, Katharine and Anna Mae Duane. 2017. *Who Writes for Black Children? African American Children's Literature Before 1900*. Minneapolis, MN: University of Minnesota Press.

Cart, Michael. 2008. 'The Value of Young Adult Literature.' *American Library Association*. www.ala.org/yalsa/guidelines/whitepapers/yalit

Cave, Roderick and Sara Ayad. 2017. *A History of Children's Books in 100 Books*. Buffalo, NY: Firefly Books.

Chambers, Aidan. 1996. *Tell Me: Children, Reading, and Talk*. Stroud, UK, Markham, Ontario: Stenhouse Publishers and Pembroke Publishers Limited.

Chevalier, Noel and Min Wild. 2013. *Reading Christopher Smart in the Twenty-first Century: 'By Succession of Delight.'* Lanham, MD: Bucknell University Press.

Clark, Beverly Lyon. 1996. *Regendering the School Story: Sassy Sissies and Tattling Tomboys*. New York: Routledge.

Clark, Beverly Lyon. 2003. *Kiddie Lit: The Cultural Construction of Children's Literature in America*. Baltimore, MD: The Johns Hopkins University Press.

Clark, Beverly Lyon and Margaret R. Higgonet. 2000. *Girls, Boys, Books, Toys: Gender in Children's Literature and Culture*. Baltimore, MD: Johns Hopkins University Press.

Coats, Karen S. 2001. 'Keepin' It Plural: Children's Studies in the Academy.' *Children's Literature Association Quarterly* 26, no. 3: 140–150.

Coats, Karen S. 2010. 'Growing Up, in Theory.' In *Handbook of Research on Children's and Young Adult Literature*, edited by Shelby A. Wolf, Karen Coats, Patricia Enciso and Christine A. Jenkins, 315–329. New York: Routledge.

Coats, Karen S. 2018. *The Bloomsbury Introduction to Children's and Young Adult Literature*. London: Bloomsbury.

Comenius, John. 1659. *Orbis Sensualium Pictus*. Translated by Charles Hoole. London: J. Kirton.

Cosslett, Tess. 2006. *Talking Animals in British Children's Fiction, 1786–1914*. Aldershot, UK, Burlington, VT: Ashgate Publishing.

Cox, Patrick. 2016. 'The Child Mechanical and Adult Anxiety in Children's Literature and Culture: "Wheels to the Rails!"' *Jeunesse: Young People, Texts, Cultures* 8, no. 2: 19–35.

Crago, Hugo. 1985. 'The Roots of Response.' *Children's Literature Association Quarterly* 10, no. 3: 100–104.

Darling, Eliza. 2001. 'The *Lorax* Redux: Profit Biggering and Some Selective Silences in American Environmentalism.' *Capitalism, Nature, Socialism* 12, no. 4: 51–66.

Darton, F.J. Harvey. [1932] 1982. *Children's Books in England: Five Centuries of Social Life*. Cambridge, UK: Cambridge University Press.

Davis, Lennard J. 1995. *Enforcing Normalcy: Disability, Deafness, and the Body*. New York: Verso.

Day, Sara K. 2013. *Reading Like a Girl: Narrative Intimacy in Contemporary American Young Adult Literature*. Jackson, MS: University Press of Mississippi.

DeRijke, Victoria. 2014. '"Creaturely Life": Biopolitical Intensity in Selected Children's Fables.' In *Politics and Ideology in Children's Literature*, edited by Marian Thérèse Keyes and Áine McGillicuddy, 45–57. Dublin: Four Courts Press.

Deszcz-Tryhubczak, Justyna. 2016. 'Using Literary Criticism for Children's Rights: Toward a Participatory Research Model of Children's Literature Studies.' *The Lion and the Unicorn* 40, no. 2: 215–231.
DiCamillo, Kate. 2013. *Flora & Ulysses: The Illuminated Adventures*. Somerville, MA: Candlewick.
Dickens, Charles. 1854. *Hard Times*. London: Bradbury and Evans.
Dine, Philip. 1997. 'The French Colonial Empire in Juvenile Fiction: From Jules Verne to Tintin.' *Historical Reflections / Réflexions Historiques* 23, no. 2: 177–203.
Dobrin, Sidney I. and Kenneth B. Kidd, eds. 2004. *Wild Things: Children's Culture and Ecocriticism*. Detroit, MI: Wayne State University Press.
Druker, Elina and Bettina Kümmerling-Meibauer. 2015. 'Introduction: Children's Literature and the Avant-Garde.' In *Children's Literature and the Avant-Garde*, edited by Elina Druker and Bettina Kümmerling-Meibauer, 1–16. Amsterdam: John Benjamins.
Duane, Anna Mae, ed. 2013. *The Children's Table: Childhood Studies and the Humanities*. Athens, GA: University of Georgia Press.
Dusinberre, Juliet. [1987] 1999. *Alice to the Lighthouse: Children's Books and Radical Experiments in Art*. New York: St. Martin's Press.
Eagleton, Terry. 1976. *Criticism and Ideology: A Study in Marxist Theory*, London: Verso.
Eagleton, Terry. 1991. *Ideology: An Introduction*. London and New York: Verso.
Echterling, Clare. 2016a. 'How to Save the World and Other Lessons from Children's Environmental Literature.' *Children's Literature in Education* 47: 283–299.
Echterling, Clare. 2016b. 'Postcolonial Ecocriticism, Classic Children's Literature, and the Imperial-Environmental Imagination in "The Chronicles of Narnia."' *The Journal of the Midwest Modern Language Association* 49, no. 1: 93–117.
Eddy, Jacalyn. 2006. *Bookwomen: Creating an Empire in Children's Book Publishing 1919–1939*. Madison, WI: University of Wisconsin Press.
Edgeworth, Maria. [1821] 1836. *Rosamond and Other Tales*. New York: Harper & Brothers.
Elick, Catherine L. 2015. *Talking Animals in Children's Fiction: A Critical Study*. Jefferson, NC: McFarland.
Eliot, T.S. 1939. *Old Possum's Book of Practical Cats*. London: Faber and Faber.
Elledge, Scott. 1984. *E.B. White: A Biography*. New York and London: Norton & Company.
Ellis, Danika Leigh. 2018. 'The 38 Best Queer YA Novels.' *Vulture*, June 21. https://www.vulture.com/2018/06/38-best-lgbtq-ya-novels.html
Farquhar, Mary Ann. 1980. 'Revolutionary Chinese Literature.' *The Australian Journal of Chinese Affairs* 4: 61–84.
Farquhar, Mary Ann. [1999] 2015. *Children's Literature in China: From Lu Xun to Mao Zedong*. New York: Routledge.
Fellman, Anita Clair. 2008. *Little House, Long Shadow: Laura Ingalls Wilder's Impact on American Culture*. Columbia, MO: University of Missouri Press.
Ferrante, Elena. 2016. *The Beach at Night*. Translated by Ann Goldstein. Illustrated by Mara Cerri. New York: Europa Editions.

Flynn, Richard. 1997. 'The Intersection of Children's Literature and Childhood Studies.' *Children's Literature Association Quarterly* 22, no. 3: 143–145.

Flynn, Richard. 2011. 'Culture.' In *Keywords for Children's Literature*, edited by Philip Nel and Lissa Paul, 62–67. New York: New York University Press.

Flynn, Richard. 2016. 'What Are We Talking About When We Talk About Agency?' *Jeunesse* 8, no. 1: 254–265.

Frénée-Hutchins, Samantha. 2016. *Boudica's Odyssey in Early Modern England*. New York: Routledge.

Ganguly, Sanghamitra. 2018. 'Reading Comics: A Post-Colonial Review of *Tintin in the Congo*.' *Veda's Journal of English Language and Literature* 5, no. 2: 102–109.

Gavin, Adrienne E. 2012. *The Child in British Literature: Literary Constructions of Childhood, Medieval to Contemporary*. New York: Palgrave Macmillan.

Glotfelty, Cheryll. 1996. 'Introduction: Literary Studies in an Age of Environmental Crisis.' In *The Ecocriticism Reader: Landmarks in Literary Ecology*, edited by Cheryll Glotfelty and Harold Fromm, xv–xxxvii. Athens, GA: University of Georgia Press.

González, Ann. 2009. *Resistance and Survival: Children's Narrative from Central America and the Caribbean*. Tucson, AZ: The University of Arizona Press.

Grenby, M.O. 2008. *Children's Literature*. Edinburgh, UK: Edinburgh University Press.

Grenby, M.O. 2011. *The Child Reader 1700–1840*. Cambridge, UK: Cambridge University Press.

Griffith, John W. 1993. *Charlotte's Web: A Pig's Salvation*. New York: Twayne Publishers.

Griswold, Jerry. 2006. *Feeling Like a Kid: Childhood and Children's Literature*. Baltimore, MD: Johns Hopkins University Press.

Gubar, Marah. 2010. *Artful Dodgers: Reconceiving the Golden Age of Children's Literature*. Oxford, UK: Oxford University Press.

Gubar, Marah. 2011. 'Theories and Methodologies: On Not Defining Children's Literature.' *PMLA* 126, no. 1: 209–216.

Gubar, Marah. 2013. 'Risky Business: Talking about Children in Children's Literature Criticism.' *Children's Literature Association Quarterly* 38, no. 4: 450–457.

Handy, Bruce. 2017a. *Wild Things: The Joy of Reading Children's Literature as an Adult*. New York: Simon & Schuster.

Handy, Bruce. 2017b. 'How "The Story of Ferdinand" Became Fodder for the Cultural Wars of Its Era.' *The New Yorker*, December 15. https://www.newyorker.com/books/page-turner/how-the-story-of-ferdinand-became-fodder-for-the-culture-wars-of-its-era

Hark, Ina Rae. 1978. 'Edward Lear: Eccentricity and Victorian Angst.' *Victorian Poetry* 16, no 1/2: 112–122.

Hawkes, David. 2004. *Ideology: The New Critical Idiom*. London: Routledge.

Hentoff, Nat. 1966. 'Among the Wild Things.' *New Yorker*, January 22, 1966: 39–73.

Hilton, Mary and Maria Nikolajeva. 2012. 'Introduction: Time of Turmoil.' In *Contemporary Adolescent Literature and Culture: The Emergent Adult*, edited by Mary Hilton and Maria Nikolajeva, 1–16. Burlington, VT: Ashgate.

Hollindale, Peter. 1997. *Signs of Childness in Children's Books*. Stroud, UK: The Thimble Press.

Honeyman, Susan. 2005. *Elusive Childhood: Impossible Representations in Modern Fiction*. Columbus, OH: The Ohio State University Press.

Honeyman, Susan. 2013. 'Trans(cending)gender through Childhood.' In *The Children's Table: Childhood Studies and the Humanities*, edited by Anna Mae Duane, 167–182. Athens, GA: University of Georgia Press.

Høyrup, Helene. 2017. 'The Origins of Modernism in Fairy Tale: Hans Christian Andersen and Canon Studies.' In *Canon Constitution and Canon Change in Children's Literature*, edited by Bettina Kümmerling-Meibauer and Anja Müller, 105–118. New York and London: Routledge.

Hunt, Nancy Rose. 2002. 'Tintin and the Interruptions of Congolese Comics.' In *Images and Empires: Visuality in Colonial and Postcolonial Africa*, edited by Paul S. Landau and Deborah D. Kaspin, 90–124. Berkeley, CA: University of California Press.

Hunt, Peter. 1991. *Criticism, Theory, & Children's Literature*. Oxford, UK: Basil Blackwell.

Hunt, Peter. 1996. 'Passing on the Past: The Problem of Books that Are for Children and That Were for Children.' *Children's Literature Association Quarterly* 21, no. 4: 200–202.

Hunt, Peter. 2011. 'Children's Literature.' In *Keywords for Children's Literature*, edited by Philip Nel and Lissa Paul, 42–48. New York and London: New York University Press.

Hutcheon, Linda, with Siobhan O'Flynn. 2013. *A Theory of Adaptation, Second Edition*. Oxford, UK: Routledge.

Jackson, Mary V. 1989. *Engines of Instruction, Mischief, and Magic: Children's Literature in England from its Beginnings to 1839*. Lincoln, NE: University of Nebraska Press.

Janeway, James. [1671] 1676. *A Token for Children: Being an Exact Account of the Conversion, Holy and Exemplary Lives, and Joyful Deaths, of several young children*. London: Dorman Newman.

Jaques, Zoe. 2015a. 'Introduction: Special Issue on Machines, Monsters and Animals: Posthumanism and Children's Literature.' *Bookbird* 53, no. 1: 4–9.

Jaques, Zoe. 2015b. *Children's Literature and the Posthuman: Animal, Environment, Cyborg*. New York: Routledge.

Jiménez García, Marilisa. 2017. 'Side-by-Side: At the Intersections of Latinx Studies and ChYALit.' *The Lion and the Unicorn* 41, no. 1: 113–122.

Joseph, Michael Scott. 1997. 'A Pre-Modernist Reading of "The Drum": Chinua Achebe and the Theme of the Eternal Return.' *ARIEL: A Review of International English Literature* 28, no 1: 149–166.

Kamenetsky, Christa. 1984. *Children's Literature in Hitler's Germany: The Cultural Policy of National Socialism*. Athens, OH: Ohio University Press.

Kaye, Frances W. 2000. 'Little Squatter on the Osage Diminished Reserve: Reading Laura Ingalls Wilder's Kansas Indians.' *Great Plains Quarterly* 20, no. 2: 123–140.

Keith, Lois. 2001. *Take Up thy Bed and Walk: Death, Disability and Cure in Classic Fiction for Girls*. New York: Routledge.

Kersten, Sara and Ashley K. Dallacqua. 2017. 'Of Studious Babes, Talking Rabbits, and Watercolor Activism: Using the Comics Form to Consider Nonfiction.' *Journal of Children's Literature* 43, no. 1: 17–26.

Kidd, Kenneth. 1998. 'Introduction: Lesbian/Gay Literature for Children and Young Adults.' *Children's Literature Association Quarterly* 23, no. 3: 114–119.

Kidd, Kenneth. 2011a. 'Queer Theory's Child and Children's Literature Studies.' *PMLA: Theories and Methodologies* 126, no. 1: 182–188.

Kidd, Kenneth. 2011b. *Freud in Oz: At the Intersections of Psychoanalysis and Children's Literature*. Minneapolis, MN: University of Minnesota Press.

Kinghorn, Norton D. 1986. 'The Real Miracle of Charlotte's Web.' *Children's Literature Association Quarterly* 11, no. 1: 4–9.

Kline, Daniel T. 2003. *Medieval Literature for Children*. New York: Routledge.

Knoepflmacher, U.C. and Mitzi Myers. 1997. 'From the Editors: "Cross-Writing" and the Reconceptualizing of Children's Literature Studies.' *Children's Literature* 25: vii–xvii.

Kümmerling-Meibauer, Bettina and Jörg Meibauer. 2013. 'Towards a Cognitive Theory of Picturebooks.' *International Research in Children's Literature* 6, no. 2: 143–160.

Kunze, Peter C. 2013. 'What We Talk about When We Talk about Helen Keller: Disabilities in Children's Biographies.' *Children's Literature Association Quarterly* 38, no. 3: 304–318.

Kutzer, M. Daphne. 2000. *Empire's Children: Empire and Imperialism in Classic British Children's Books*. New York: Routledge.

Lamb, Edel. 2010. 'The Literature of Early Modern Childhoods.' *Literature Compass* 7/6: 412–423.

Lamb, Edel. 2012. '"Children read for their Pleasantness": Books for Schoolchildren in the Seventeenth Century.' In *The Child in British Literature: Literary Constructions of Childhood, Medieval to Contemporary*, edited by Adrienne E. Gavin, 69–83. New York: Palgrave Macmillan.

Lear, Edward. [1846] 1875. *A Book of Nonsense*. New York: James Miller.

Lee and Low. [2013]. 'Why Hasn't the Number of Multicultural Books Increased in Eighteen Years?' June 17. https://blog.leeandlow.com/2013/06/17/why-hasnt-the-number-of-multicultural-books-increased-in-eighteen-years/

Lee and Low. 2016. 'Where is the Diversity in Publishing? The 2015 Diversity Baseline Survey Results.' January 26. https://blog.leeandlow.com/2016/01/26/where-is-the-diversity-in-publishing-the-2015-diversity-baseline-survey-results/

Lefebvre, Benjamin, ed. 2013.*Textual Transformations in Children's Literature: Adaptations, Translations, Reconsiderations*. New York: Routledge.

LeGuin, Ursula. 2004. 'Cheek by Jowl: Animals in Children's Literature.' *Children and Libraries*, Summer/Fall: 20–30.

Lenzer, Gertrud. 2001. 'Childhood Studies: Beginnings and Purposes.' *The Lion and the Unicorn* 25, no. 2: 181–186.

Lerer, Seth. 2008. *Children's Literature: A Reader's History, from Aesop to Harry Potter.* Chicago, IL: University of Chicago Press.

Lesnik-Oberstein, Karin. 1998. 'Children's Literature and the Environment.' In *Writing the Environment: Ecocriticism and Literature*, edited by Richard Kerridge and Neil Sammells, 208–217. New York: Zed Books.

Lesnik-Oberstein, Karin, ed. 2004. *Children's Literature: New Approaches.* New York: Palgrave Macmillan.

Levy, Michael and Farah Mendlesohn. 2016. *Children's Fantasy Literature: An Introduction.* Cambridge, UK: Cambridge University Press.

Lewis, C.S. [1956] 1994. *The Last Battle.* New York: Harper/Trophy.

Lodge, Sara. 2016. 'Edward Lear and Dissent.' In *Edward Lear and the Play of Poetry*, edited by James Williams and Matthew Bevis, 70–89. Oxford, UK: Oxford University Press.

Lundin, Anne. 2004. *Constructing the Canon of Children's Literature: Beyond Library Walls and Ivory Towers.* New York and London: Routledge.

Lurie, Alison. 1990. *Don't Tell the Grown-Ups: Subversive Children's Literature.* Boston, MA: Little, Brown.

MacCann, Donnarae. 2001. *White Supremacy in Children's Literature: Characterizations of African Americans, 1830–1900.* New York: Routledge.

Mackey, Margaret. 2010. 'Reading from the Feet Up: The Local Work of Literacy.' *Children's Literature in Education* 41, no. 4: 323–339.

Mackey, Margaret. 2016. *One Child Reading: My Auto-Bibliography.* Edmonton, Alberta: The University of Alberta Press.

Mallan, Kerry. 2013. 'Empathy: Narrative Empathy and Children's Literature.' In *(Re)imagining the World: Children's Literature's Response to Changing Times*, edited by Yan Wu, Kerry Mallan and Roderick McGillis, 105–114. Heidelberg, Germany: Springer.

Marlin, Randal. 2013. *Propaganda and the Ethics of Persuasion*, 2nd ed. Peterborough, Ontario: Broadview Press.

Marshall, H.E. 1905. *Our Island Story: A History of England for Boys and Girls.* London: T.C. and E.C. Jack.

Marshall, Ian S. 1996. 'The Lorax and the Ecopolice.' *ISLE: Interdisciplinary Studies in Literature and Environment* 2, no. 2: 85–92.

Martin, Michelle. 2004. *Brown Gold: Milestones of African American Children's Picture Books, 1845–2002.* New York: Routledge.

McCallum, Robyn. 1999. *Ideologies of Identity in Adolescent Fiction: The Dialogic Construction of Subjectivity.* New York: Taylor & Francis.

McCallum, Robyn and John Stephens. 2011. 'Ideology and Children's Books.' In *Handbook of Research on Children's Literature*, edited by Shelby A. Wolf, Karen Coats, Patricia Enciso and Christine A. Jenkins, 359–372. New York: Routledge.

McCarthy, William. 2005. 'Mother of All Discourses: Anna Barbauld's *Lessons for Children.*' In *Culturing the Child, 1690–1914: Essays in Memory of Mitzi Myers*, edited by Donelle Ruwe, 85–113. Lanham, MD: Scarecrow Press.

McDowell, Myles. 1973. 'Fiction for Children and Adults: Some Essential Differences.' *Children's Literature in Education* 10, vol. 4, no. 1: 50–63.
McGavran, James Holt Jr. and Jennifer Smith Daniel. 2012. 'Introduction.' In *Time of Beauty, Time of Fear: The Romantic Legacy in the Literature of Childhood*, edited by James McGavran, xi–xxv. Iowa City, IA: University of Iowa Press.
McGillis, Roderick. 1996. *The Nimble Reader*. New York: Twayne Publishers.
McGillis, Roderick. 2002. 'Getting What We Want: The Politics of Identity in Three Vigils.' *Children's Literature in Education* 33, no. 1: 1–10.
McGillis, Roderick. 2009. 'What is Children's Literature?' *Children's Literature* 37: 256–262.
McGillis, Roderick and Meena Khorana. 1997. 'Postcolonialism, Children, and their Literature.' *ARIEL: A Review of International English Literature* 28, no. 1: 7–20.
Mickenberg, Julia L. 2005. *Learning from the Left: Children's Literature, The Cold War, and Radical Politics in the United States*. Oxford, UK: Oxford University Press.
Mickenberg, Julia L. 2017. 'Radical Children's Literature'. *Oxford Research Encyclopedia of Literature*. New York: Oxford University Press. http://literature.oxfordre.com/view/10.1093/acrefore/9780190201098.001.0001/acrefore-9780190201098-e-89
Mickenberg, Julia L. and Lynne Vallone, eds. 2011. *The Oxford Handbook of Children's Literature*. Oxford, UK: Oxford University Press.
Miller, Laura. 2008. *The Magician's Book: A Skeptic's Adventures in Narnia*. New York: Little, Brown and Company.
Mills, Claudia. 2014. 'Children's Books Should Avoid Propaganda.' *The New York Times Opinion Pages: Room for Debate*, July 9. https://www.nytimes.com/roomfordebate/2014/07/09/should-books-for-childrens-be-political/childrens-books-should-avoid-propaganda
Mitchell, David T. and Sharon L. Snyder. 2000. *Narrative Prosthesis: Disability and the Dependencies of Discourse*. Ann Arbor, MI: University of Michigan Press.
Morgan, Judith and Neil Morgan. 1995. *Dr. Seuss & Mr. Geisel*. New York: Random House.
Moruzi, Kristine. 2018. 'Charity, Affect, and Waif Novels.' In *Affect, Emotion, and Children's Literature: Representation and Socialisation in Texts for Children and Young Adults*, edited by Kristine Moruzi, Michelle J. Smith and Elizabeth Bullen, 33–52. New York: Routledge.
Myers, Mitzi. 1989. 'Socializing Rosamond: Educational Ideology and Fictional Form.' *Children's Literature Association Quarterly* 14, no. 2: 52–58.
Myers, Walter Dean. 2014. 'Where Are the People of Color in Children's Books?' *New York Times Opinion*, March 15. https://www.nytimes.com/2014/03/16/opinion/sunday/where-are-the-people-of-color-in-childrens-books.html
Naidoo, Jamie Campbell and Sarah Park Dahlen. 2013. *Diversity in Youth Literature: Opening Doors through Reading*. Chicago, IL: American Library Association Editions.
Nance-Carroll, Niall. 2014. 'Innocence is No Defense: Politicized Childhood in Antonio Skármeta's La composición/The Composition.' *Children's Literature in Education* 45, no. 4: 271–284.

Nel, Philip. 2011. 'Ferdinand at 75.' *Nine Kinds of Pie*. September 17. Blog available at: http://www.philnel.com/2011/09/17/ferdinand/

Nel, Philip. 2017. *Was the Cat in the Hat Black?* Oxford, UK: Oxford University Press.

Nelson, Claudia. 1998. 'David and Jonathan—and Saul—Revisited: Homodomestic Patterns in British Boys' Magazine Fiction, 1880–1915.' *Children's Literature Association Quarterly* 23, no. 3: 120–127.

Neubauer, John. 1992. *The Fin-de-Siècle Culture of Adolescence*. New Haven, CT: Yale University Press.

Nikolajeva, Maria. 2014. *Reading for Learning: Cognitive Approaches to Children's Literature*. Amsterdam: John Benjamins.

Nikolajeva, Maria. [1996] 2016. *Children's Literature Comes of Age: Toward a New Aesthetic*. New York: Routledge.

Nikolajeva, Maria. 2016. 'Recent Trends in Children's Literature Research: Return to the Body.' *International Research in Children's Literature* 9, no. 2: 132–145.

Nodelman, Perry. 1992. 'The Other: Orientalism, Colonialism, and Children's Literature.' *Children's Literature Association Quarterly* 17, no. 1: 29–35.

Nodelman, Perry. 2008. *The Hidden Adult: Defining Children's Literature*. Baltimore, MD: The Johns Hopkins University Press.

Nodelman, Perry. 2013. 'The Disappearing Childhood of Children's Literature Studies.' *Jeunesse: Young People, Texts, Cultures* 5, no. 1: 149–163.

Nodelman, Perry and Mavis Reimer. 2003. *The Pleasures of Children's Literature*. New York: Pearson.

O'Dell, Felicity Ann. 1978. *Socialisation Through Children's Literature: The Soviet Example*. Cambridge, UK: Cambridge University Press.

O'Malley, Andrew. 2004. *The Making of the Modern Child: Children's Literature in the Late Eighteenth Century*. New York: Routledge.

O'Malley, Andrew. 2012. 'Crusoe's Children: *Robinson Crusoe* and the Culture of Childhood in the Eighteenth Century.' In *The Child in British Literature: Literary Constructions of Childhood, Medieval to Contemporary*, edited by Adrienne E. Gavin, 87–100. New York: Palgrave Macmillan.

op de Beeck, Nathalie. 2010. *Suspended Animation: Children's Picture Books and the Fairy Tale of Modernity*. Minneapolis, MN: University of Minnesota Press.

Orme, Nicholas. 2006. *Medieval Schools: From Roman Britain to Renaissance England*. New Haven, CT: Yale University Press.

Ostry, Elaine. 2002. *Social Dreaming: Dickens and the Fairy Tale*. New York: Routledge.

Ostry, Elaine. 2004. '"Is He Still Human? Are You?": Young Adult Science Fiction in the Posthuman Age.' *The Lion and the Unicorn* 28, no. 2: 222–246.

O'Sullivan, Emer. 2005a. *Comparative Children's Literature*. Oxford and New York: Routledge.

O'Sullivan, Emer. 2005b. 'Theories and Methodologies: Comparative Children's Literature.' *PMLA* 126, no. 1: 189–196.

Oziewicz, Marek C. 2015. *Justice in Young Adult Speculative Fiction: A Cognitive Reading*. New York: Routledge.

Paul, Lissa. 1987. 'Enigma Variations: What Feminist Theory Knows about Children's Literature.' *Signal* 54: 186–202.

Pinsent, Pat. 2017. '"Making Disciples of the Young": Children's Literature and Religion.' In *The Bloomsbury Reader in Religion and Childhood*, edited by Anna Strhan, Stephen G. Parker and Susan B. Ridgely, 247–259. New York: Bloomsbury.

Pleasants, Kathleen. 2006. 'Does Environmental Education Need a Thneed? Displacing The Lorax as Environmental Text.' *Canadian Journal of Environmental Education* 11: 179–194.

Postman, Neil. [1982] 1994. *The Disappearance of Childhood*. New York: Vintage/Random House.

Ratelle, Amy. 2015. *Animality and Children's Literature and Film*. Basingstoke, UK: Palgrave Macmillan.

Resene, Michelle. 2016. 'A "Curious Incident": Representations of Autism in Children's Detective Fiction.' *The Lion and the Unicorn* 40, no. 1: 81–99.

Reynolds, Kimberley. 1990. *Girls Only?: Gender and Popular Children's Fiction in Britain, 1880–1910*. Philadelphia, PA: Temple University Press.

Reynolds, Kimberley. 2007. *Radical Children's Literature: Future Visions and Aesthetic Transformations in Juvenile Fiction*. New York: Palgrave Macmillan.

Reynolds, Kimberley. 2011. *Children's Literature. A Very Short Introduction*. Oxford, UK: Oxford University Press.

Reynolds, Kimberley. 2016. *Left Out: The Forgotten Tradition of Radical Publishing for Children in Britain 1910–1949*. Oxford, UK: Oxford University Press.

Richardson, Alan. 2006. 'Cognitive Literary Criticism.' In *Literary Theory and Criticism: An Oxford Guide*, edited by Patricia Waugh, 544–556. Oxford, UK: Oxford University Press.

Rickert, Edith, ed. 1908. *The Babees' Book: Medieval Manners for the Young: Done into Modern English from Dr. Furnivall's Texts*. London: Chatto & Windus.

Rieder, John. 1998. 'Edward Lear's Limericks: The Function of Children's Nonsense Poetry.' *Children's Literature* 26: 47–60.

Rioux, Anne Boyd. 2018. *Meg, Jo, Beth, Amy: The Story of Little Women and Why It Still Matters*. New York: W.W. Norton.

Robinson, Laura. 2004. 'Bosom Friends: Lesbian Desire in L.M. Montgomery's Anne Books.' *Canadian Literature* 180: 12–28.

Robinson, Peter. 2016. 'Edward Lear: Celebrity Chef.' In *Edward Lear and the Play of Poetry*, edited by James Williams and Matthew Bevis, 115–134. Oxford, UK: Oxford University Press.

Romines, Ann. 1990. '*The Long Winter*: An Introduction to Western Womanhood.' *Great Plains Quarterly* 503: 36–47.

Rose, Jacqueline. [1984] 1992. *The Case of Peter Pan, or The Impossibility of Children's Fiction, Revised Edition*. London: The Macmillan Press.

Rouleau, Brian. 2016. '"In Praise of Trash": Series Fiction Fan Mail and the Challenges of Children's Devotion.' *The Journal of the History of Childhood and Youth* 9, no. 3: 403–423.

Rubin, Ellen and Emily Strauss Watson. 1987. 'Disability Bias in Children's Literature.' *The Lion and the Unicorn* 11, no. 1: 60–67.
Rudd, David. 2010. 'Children's Literature and the Return to Rose.' *Children's Literature Association Quarterly* 35, no. 3: 290–310.
Rudd, David. 2013. *Reading the Child in Children's Literature: An Heretical Approach.* Basingstoke, UK: Palgrave Macmillan.
Rudd, David and Anthony Pavlik. 2010. 'The (Im)Possibility of Children's Fiction: Rose Twenty-Five Years On.' *Children's Literature Association Quarterly* 35, no. 3: 223–229.
Rule, Stacy. 2011. 'Animal Meaning in T. S. Eliot's *Old Possum's Book of Practical Cats*.' In *Making Animal Meaning*, edited by Linda Kalof and Georgina M. Montgomery, 145–158. East Lansing, MI: Michigan State University Press.
Russo, Maria. 2016. 'Elena Ferrante's Picture Book Embraces the Dark Side.' *The New York Times*, 12 October: BR23.
Ruys, Juanita Feros. 2018. 'From Virtue Ethics to Emotional Intelligence: Advice from Medieval Parents to Their Children.' In *Affect, Emotion, and Children's Literature: Representation and Socialisation in Texts for Children and Young Adults*, edited by Kristine Moruzi, Michelle J. Smith and Elizabeth Bullen, 19–32. New York: Routledge.
Sánchez-Eppler, Karen. 2011. 'Marks of Possession: Methods for an Impossible Subject.' *PMLA* 126, no. 1: 151–159.
Sánchez-Eppler, Karen. 2013. 'In the Archives of Childhood.' In *The Children's Table: Childhood Studies and the Humanities*, edited by Anna Mae Duane, 213–237. Athens, GA: University of Georgia Press.
Sands-O'Connor, Karen. 2014. 'Introduction: Stepping Out into the World: Series and Internationalism.' In *Internationalism in Children's Series*, edited by Karen Sands-O'Connor and Marietta A. Frank, 1–19. Basingstoke, UK: Palgrave Macmillan.
Saunders, Kathy. 2004. 'What Disability Studies Can Do for Children's Literature.' *Disability Studies Quarterly* 24, no. 1. http://dx.doi.org/10.18061/dsq.v24i1.849
Schey, Ryan. 2017. 'Toward Intersectional Literary Practices: Interrogating Homonormativity through Reading Sáenz's *Aristotle and Dante*.' *The Alan Review* 45, no.1: 32–43.
Schwebel, Sara L. 2011. *Child-Sized History: Fictions of the Past in U.S. Classrooms.* Nashville, TN: Vanderbilt University Press.
Schwebel, Sara L. 2016. 'The Limits of Agency for Children's Literature Scholars.' *Jeunesse: Young People, Texts, Cultures* 8, no. 1: 278–290.
Sciurba, Katie. 2017. 'Flowers, Dancing, Dresses, and Dolls: Picture Book Representations of Gender-Variant Males.' *Children's Literature in Education* 48: 276–293.
Seuss, Dr. [Theodor Geisel] 1971. *The Lorax.* New York: Random House.
Sigler, Caroline. 1994. 'Wonderland to Wasteland: Toward Historicizing Environmental Activism in Children's Literature.' *Children's Literature Association Quarterly* 19, no. 4: 148–153.

Silvey, Anita, ed. 2002. *The Essential Guide to Children's Books and Their Creators.* New York: Mariner Books.

Skármeta, Antonio. 2003. Illustrated by Alfonso Ruano. *The Composition.* Toronto, Ontario: Groundwood Books.

Smith-D'Arezzo, Wendy and Janine Holc. 2016. 'Reframing Disability through Graphic Novels for Girls: Alternative Bodies in Cece Bell's El Deafo.' *Girlhood Studies* 9, no. 1: 72–87.

Snell, Heather. 2017. 'Childhood, Children's Literature, and Postcolonialism.' *Jeunesse: Young People, Texts, Cultures* 9, no. 1: 176–187.

Sommerville, C. John. 1992. *The Discovery of Childhood in Puritan England.* Athens, GA: The University of Georgia Press.

Spufford, Francis. 2002. *The Child that Books Built: A Life in Reading.* London: Faber & Faber.

Steiner, Evgeny. 1999. *Stories for Little Comrades: Revolutionary Artists and the Making of Early Soviet Children's Books.* Seattle, WA: University of Washington Press.

Stephens, John. 1992. *Language and Ideology in Children's Fiction.* London and New York: Longman.

Teorey, Matthew. 2014. 'The Lorax and Wallace Stegner: Inspiring Children's Environmental Activism.' *Children's Literature in Education* 45, no. 4: 324–339.

Thein, Amanda Haertling and Kate E. Kedley. 2016. 'Out of the Closet and All Grown Up: Problematizing Normative Narratives of Coming-Out and Coming-of-Age in Young Adult Literature.' In *Beyond Borders: queer eros and ethos (ethics) in LGBTQ young adult literature*, edited by Darla Linville and David Lee Carlson, 3–20. New York: Peter Lang.

Thomas, Ebony Elizabeth. 2018. 'Toward a Theory of the Dark Fantastic: The Role of Racial Difference in Young Adult Speculative Fiction and Media.' *Journal of Language and Literacy Education* 14, no. 1: 1–10.

Thomas, Ebony Elizabeth, Debbie Reese and Kathleen T. Horning. 2016. 'Much Ado about *A Fine Dessert*: The Cultural Politics of Representing Slavery in Children's Literature.' *Journal of Children's Literature* 42, no 2: 6–17.

Thomas, Joyce. 1985. '"There Was an Old Man...": The Sense of Nonsense Verse.' *Children's Literature Association Quarterly* 10, no. 3: 119–122.

Thomson-Wohlgemuth, Gabriele. 2003. 'Children's Literature and Translation Under the East German Regime.' *Meta* 48, no. 1–2: 241–249.

Tougaw, Jason. 2018. *The Elusive Brain: Literary Experiments in the Age of Neuroscience.* New Haven, CT, and London: Yale University Press.

Townsend, John. 1980. 'Standards of Criticism for Children's Literature.' In *The Signal Approach to Children's Books*, edited by Nancy Chambers, 193–207. Metuchen, NJ, and London: Scarecrow Books.

Travisano, Thomas. 2000. 'Of Dialectic and Divided Consciousness: Intersections Between Children's Literature and Childhood Studies.' *Children's Literature* 28: 22–29.

Tribunella, Eric L. 2004. 'A Boy and His Dog: Canine Companions and the Proto-Erotics of Youth.' *Children's Literature Association Quarterly* 29, no. 3: 152–171.

Tribunella, Eric L. 2010. *Melancholia and Maturation: The Use of Trauma in American Children's Literature*. Knoxville, TN: University of Tennessee Press.
Tribunella, Eric L. 2012. 'Between Boys: Edward Stevenson's *Left to Themselves* (1891) and the Birth of Gay Children's Literature.' *Children's Literature Association Quarterly* 37, no. 4: 374–388.
Trites, Roberta Seelinger. 1998. 'Queer Discourse and the Young Adult Novel: Repression and Power in Gay Male Adolescent Literature.' *Children's Literature Association Quarterly* 23, no. 3: 143–151.
Trites, Roberta Seelinger. 2004. *Disturbing the Universe: Power and Repression in Adolescent Literature*. Iowa City, IA: University of Iowa Press.
Trites, Roberta Seelinger. 2007a. 'Review of *Feeling Like a Kid*: Childhood and Children's Literature.' *Children's Literature Association Quarterly* 32, no. 4: 394–397.
Trites, Roberta Seelinger. 2007b. *Twain, Alcott, and the Birth of the Adolescent Reform Novel*. Iowa City, IA: University of Iowa Press.
Trites, Roberta Seelinger. 2014. *Literary Conceptualizations of Growth: Metaphors and Cognition in Adolescent Literature*. Amsterdam: John Benjamins.
Trites, Roberta Seelinger. 2018. *Twenty-First-Century Feminisms in Children's and Adolescent Literature*. Jackson, MS: University Press of Mississippi.
Ulaby, Neda. 2015. '"George" Wants You to Know: She's Really Melissa.' *NPR Morning Edition*, August 27. https://www.npr.org/2015/08/27/434277989/-george-wants-you-to-know-she-s-really-melissa
Vaclavik, Kiera. 2011. 'Goodbye, Ghetto: Further Comparative Approaches to Children's Literature.' *PMLA* 126, no. 1: 203–208.
Wall, Barbara. 1991. *The Narrator's Voice: The Dilemma of Children's Fiction*. New York: Palgrave Macmillan.
Wall, John. 2013. 'Childism: The Challenge of Childhood to Ethics and the Humanities.' In *The Children's Table: Childhood Studies and the Humanities*, edited by Anna Mae Duane, 69–84. Athens, GA: University of Georgia Press.
Wannamaker, Annette. 2008. *Boys in Children's Literature and Popular Culture: Masculinity, Abjection, and the Fictional Child*. New York: Taylor & Francis.
Westman, Karin E. 2007. 'Children's Literature and Modernism: The Space Between.' *Children's Literature Association Quarterly* 32, no 4: 283–286.
Westman, Karin E. 2013. 'Beyond Periodization: Children's Literature, Genre, and Remediating Literary History.' *Children's Literature Association Quarterly* 38, no. 4: 464–469.
Wetta, Molly. 2013. 'What is New Adult Fiction, Anyway?' *NoveList*. https://www.ebscohost.com/novelist/novelist-special/what-is-new-adult-fiction-anyway
White, E.B. [1952] 1980. *Charlotte's Web*. New York: Harper Collins.
Whitley, David. 2013. 'Contested Spaces: Reconfiguring Narratives of Origin and Identity in *Pocahontas* and *Princess Mononoke*,' In *Textual Transformations in Children's Literature: Adaptations, Translations, Reconsiderations*, edited by Benjamin Lefebvre, 7–21. New York: Routledge.
Wilder, Laura Ingalls. [1935]1971. *Little House on the Prairie*. New York: Harper Trophy.

Williams, Abigail. 2017. *The Social Life of Books: Reading Together in the Eighteenth-Century Home*. New Haven, CT: Yale University Press.

Williams, James. 2016. 'Lear and the Fool.' In *Edward Lear and the Play of Poetry*, edited by James Williams and Matthew Bevis, 16–51. Oxford, UK: Oxford University Press.

Wimsatt, W.K. and Monroe Beardsley. 1946. 'The Intentional Fallacy.' *The Sewanee Review* 54, no. 3: 468–488.

Woodside, Christine. 2016. *Libertarians on the Prairie: Laura Ingalls Wilder, Rose Wilder Lane, and the Making of the Little House Books*. New York: Arcade Publishing.

Xu, Xu. 2011. '"Chairman Mao's Child": Sparkling Red Star and the Construction of Children in the Chinese Cultural Revolution.' *Children's Literature Association Quarterly* 36, no. 4: 381–409.

Zipes, Jack. 2001. *Sticks and Stones: The Troublesome Success of Children's Literature from Slovenly Peter to Harry Potter*. New York: Routledge.

INDEX

Abate, Michelle Ann 82, 88
ableism 86, 129
Absolutely True Diary of a Part-Time Indian, The 130
Achebe, Chinua 141–142
Adams, Gillian 42, 44, 48, 56
Adams, Richard 10, 137, 148–149
adolescence 31–34
adult readers 6, 14, 22, 72–73
Adventures of a Pincushion, The 129
Aesop 47, 79
affect theory 110–111
age leveling 6, 43
Akata Witch 71–72
Albertalli, Becky 125
Alcott, Louisa May 52, 128
Alexie, Sherman 130
Alice's Adventures in Wonderland 62
Althusser, Louis 85
Andersen, Hans Christian 70
Anderson, M. T. 84
Ang, Susan 80, 81, 82
Anglocentrism 118
Animal Farm 147
animal satire 90
animal studies 136, 146–152
Anne of Green Gables 124
anthropomorphism 137, 147, 148
Ariès, Philippe 45
Ascham, Roger 51
Asim, Jabari 89
As You Like It 46
avant-garde movements 63–64
Ayad, Sara 53, 54, 55, 141

Babees' Book, The 49
Bahktin, Mikhail 24, 78, 83; and carnivalesque 83; dialogism 24; heteroglossia 78

Bailey, Merridee L. 49
Balibar, Étienne 77–78
Barbauld, Anna Laetitia 55, 57
Barrie, J.M. 128
Baskin, Barbara H. 130
Batty, Holly 151
Bavidge, Jenny 143
Beach at Night, The 18
Beardsley, Monroe 12
Beck, Julie 33
Bell, Cece 104–105, 132–135, 155
Bennett, William J. 88
Bernstein, Robin 115, 157
Bérubé, Michael 131
BFG, The 18
Bishop, Rudine Sims 113
Black Arts Movement 115
Black Beauty 62, 149
Blackford, Holly 120
Bluebond-Langner, Myra 38
Blume, Judy 29
Book for Boys and Girls, A 53
Book of Nonsense, A 42, 72
Book of Virtues, The 88
Boreman, Thomas 54
Bows Against the Barons 87
Boy Meets Boy 124
boy readers 121–122
Bradford, Clare 86, 98, 139, 140, 141, 142
Brown, Margaret Wise 66, 67–68
Bullen, Elizabeth 110, 111
Bunyan, John 52, 53
Burnett, Frances Hodgson 62, 63, 84

capitalism 16, 81 *see also* commercialism
Capshaw, Katharine 117
Carroll, Lewis 11, 62, 157

Cart, Michael 32
The Catcher in the Rye 32
Cave, Roderick 53, 54, 55, 141
Chambers, Aidan 25
Charlie and the Chocolate Factory 86, 140
Charlotte's Web 36–40, 122, 137, 154
Chaucer, Geoffrey 47
Chevalier, Noel 55
child agency 3, 152, 155
child development 16
childhood 26, 45–46, 47, 89–90, 103–104, 106; and agency 3, 152, 155; and innocence 8, 15, 19, 21, 23, 156
childhood studies 36, 103, 105–106
childism 108
childist criticism 25
children's literature, definitions of 7–36
Cinq semaines en ballon 138
Civil Rights Movement 115, 117
Clark, Beverly Lyon 35, 63
classical period 43–44
Coats, Karen 32, 36, 105
cognitive literary criticism 103, 105, 108–113
colonialism 102, 114, 138–139, 140–142; and childhood 139
Comenius, John 41, 50
coming-out narrative 125–126
commercialization 30, 54–55, 56, 69–70, 81, 88–89
comparative children's literature 69–72
Composition, The 20
Coolidge, Susan 129
Cooper, Mary 54
Cosslett, Tess 148, 149, 150
courtesy books 47, 49, 157
Cox, Patrick 65
Crago, Hugh 25
Cultural Revolution 92, 94
Curious Incident of the Dog in the Night-Time, The 112

Dahlen, Sarah Park 27
Dahl, Roald 18, 86, 140

Dallacqua, Ashley K. 133
Darius the Great is Not Okay 121
Darling, Eliza 145
Darton, F.J. Harvey 11, 62
Davis, Lennard J. 127
Day, Sara K. 120
Deaf community 134
decolonization 114, 136
Defoe, Daniel 60
DeRijke, Victoria 47, 80
Deszcz-Tryhubczak, Justyna 107
DiCamillo, Kate 137, 138, 152–155
Dickens, Charles 62–63, 106
didacticism 49–50, 73, 93
Dine, Philip 138
disability 104, 113, 127–132, 154–155; and diagnosis 130–131; models of 127–128; stereotypes 130
discourse 126
diversity 13, 104, 115, 116
Dobrin, Sidney 142–143
Doderer, Klaus 69
Draper, Sharon 128
Dream Keeper, The 118
Druker, Elina 64
Duane, Anna Mae 105, 106–107
Dusinberre, Juliet 64
Duyvis, Corinne 116

Eagleton, Terry 84, 85, 98
early modern children's literature 51–52
East Germany 92, 93
Echterling, Clare 143–144
ecocriticism 136, 142–146
Eddy, Jaclyn 35
Edgeworth, Maria 57, 58, 59, 82; and Richard Edgeworth 57, 58
eighteenth century children's literature 54–55, 80
El Deafo 104–105, 132–135, 155
Elick, Catherine 148
Eliot, T. S. 147–148
Elledge, Scott 39
embourgeoisement 11, 55, 81
Émile, or On Education 60

empathy 111
empire 114, 140
Equiano, Olaudah 27
Eurocentrism 114, 118, 141–142
Evangelical movement 57
Extremely Loud & Incredibly Close 45

fables 42, 137, 146–147
fan fiction 30
Farquhar, Mary Ann 41, 71, 94
Fauconnier, Gilles 109
Fault in our Stars, The 53
Fellman, Anita Clair 100
feminism 120, 124–126, 152; and intersectionality 120
'Fern Hill' 106, 107
Ferrante, Elena 18–19
Fielding, Sarah 56
Flora and Ulysses: The Illuminated Adventures 137, 152–155
Flynn, Richard 3, 5
Foer, Jonathan Safran 45
Frénée-Hutchins, Samantha 102
Freud, Sigmund 23, 36, 123
From Nowhere to the North Pole 8

Ganguly, Sanghamitra 92
Gantos, Jack 131
Gavin, Adrienne 45–46, 57
gender 3, 15, 62, 97, 101, 104, 114, 120–126, 153
George 122
Gino, Alex 122
girl readers 120
global histories 41, 68–72, 140–141, 158
Glotfelty, Cheryll 142
golden age 8, 11, 62, 81
González, Ann 19–20, 156–157
Goodnight Moon 66, 68
Governess, The 56
Grahame, Kenneth 148
Green, John 53
Grenby, M.O. 15, 55, 120
Griffith, John W. 38
Griswold, Jerry 26

Grossman, Lev 2
Gubar, Marah 7–8, 9, 13, 24, 156

Haddon, Mark 112
Hall, G. Stanley 31
Handy, Bruce 91
Hard Times 62–63
Hark, Ina Rae 72
Harlem Renaissance 118, 119
Harris, Karen H. 130
Harry Potter series 6, 30–31, 151, 157
Hawkes, David 81
Hazard, Paul 69
Heidi 130
Hergé (Georges Prosper Remi) 91
heteronormativity 114
heterosexism 114
Hilton, Mary 31–32, 33
Holc, Janine 104, 133, 135
Hollindale, Peter 14, 22, 89–90
homophobia 86
Honeyman, Susan 28, 122
Hood, Tom 8
Horning, Kathleen T. 115
Høyrup, Helene 70
Huckleberry Finn 35
Hughes, Langston 118
Hughes, Thomas 44, 62, 124
human–animal relationship 39, 136–137, 138, 148–152, 154
Hunt, Nancy Rose 91
Hunt, Peter 4, 10, 25, 46, 48, 69, 108
Hurd, Clement 66
Hutcheon, Linda 13

ideology 77, 84–86, 95, 100
Indigeneity 101, 118, 136
intentional fallacy 12
interdisciplinarity 4, 5, 34–36, 103, 105, 158
internationalism 68–72
intersectionality 120, 125, 126

Jackson, Mary V. 55–56, 58
Janeway, James 52–53

Jaques, Zoe 151
Jiménez García, Marilisa 118–119
Joey Pigza Swallowed the Key 131
Joseph, Michael Scott 140

Kamenetsky, Christa 93
Kaye, Frances W. 98, 115
Kedley, Kate E. 125
Keller, Helen 128
Kersten, Sara 133
Khan, Sabina 126
Khorana, Meena 139, 141
Khorram, Adib 121
Kidd, Kenneth 36, 122, 124
Kilner, Mary Jane 129
Kinghorn, Norton D. 37
kinship model 24
Klassen, Jon 150
Kline, Daniel T. 46, 48–49
Kümmerling-Meibauer, Bettina 64, 110
Kunze, Peter 128
Kutzer, M. Daphne 139, 140

Lamb, Edel 41, 51–52
Lane, Rose Wilder 79, 99
Larrick, Nancy 115
Leaf, Munro 90
Lear, Edward 42, 72–75, 157
Lee, Amanda 134
Lee and Low 116
Lefebvre, Benjamin 99, 101
LeGuin, Ursula 90, 148
Lenzer, Gertrud 105
Lerer, Seth 43, 52, 54, 79–80
Lesnik-Oberstein, Karin 35, 146
Levithan, David 124
Levy, Michael 43–44, 67
Lewis, C. S. 1, 2, 10, 22, 28, 144
LGBTQ+ literature 124–126
Lion, the Witch and the Wardrobe, The 1, 2, 10, 22
literacy narrative 5
literary periods 65–68
Little House on the Prairie series 79, 97–102

Little Pretty Pocketbook, A 55, 56
Little Women 35, 52, 121, 128
Locke, John 54, 106
Lodge, Sara 73
Lorax, The 145–146
Loves and Lies of Rukhsana Ali, The 126
Lundin, Anne 35, 61, 63, 83
Lurie, Alison 26, 83

MacCann, Donnarae 114
Macherey, Pierre 77–78
Mackey, Margaret 5, 27, 95
Magician's Trilogy, The 2
Mallan, Kerry 111
Marcus, Leonard 68
Marlin, Randal 92
Marshall, H. E. (Helen Elizabeth) 79, 101–102
Marshall, Ian S. 96
Martin, Michelle 118
Mary Poppins 150
McCallum, Robyn 77, 78, 85
McCarthy, William 55
McDowell, Myles 9–10, 11
McGavran, James Holt Jr. 60, 61
McGillis, Roderick 7, 15, 59, 82, 139, 140
medieval children's literature 44, 47–49
Meibauer, Jörg 110
Mendlesohn, Farah 43–44, 67
Mickenberg, Julia L. 19, 87
middle class 11–12, 55, 81
Miller, Laura 1, 2, 22, 27
Mills, Claudia 89
'Mirrors, Windows and Sliding Doors' 113
Mitchell, David T. 129, 154
modernism 63–65; and Hans Christian Andersen 70
Montgomery, L. M. 124
More, Hannah 57
Moruzi, Kristine 80, 110, 111
Myers, Christopher 116
Myers, Mitzi 48, 58
Myers, Walter Dean 115, 116

Naidoo, Jamie Campbell 27
Nance-Carroll, Niall 21
narrative prosthesis 129, 154
Nazi Germany 92, 93
Nel, Philip 86, 90, 116, 117
Neubauer, John 31
Newbery John 55, 56
niche publications 88
Nikolajeva, Maria 14, 31–32, 33, 34–35, 52, 109–110, 112, 126, 130
Nodelman, Perry 8–9, 15, 16–17, 19, 81, 82–83, 139, 140
nonsense 72–75, 157
nostalgia 26

Okorafor, Nnedi 71–72, 118
Old Possum's Book of Practical Cats 147–148
O'Malley, Andrew 54, 56, 60
Op de Beeck, Nathalie 64–65
Orbis Sensualium Pictus 41, 50
Orme, Nicholas 46–47
Orwell, George 147
Ostry, Elaine 56–57, 150
O'Sullivan, Emer 21, 35, 69, 70–71
OwnVoices 116–117
Our Island Story 79, 101–102
Out of My Mind 128
Oziewicz, Marek C 111

Palacio, R. J. 130
Panchatantra 47
pastoral 84, 85, 143
Pavlik, Anthony 23
Pax 150
Pennypacker, Sara 150
Peter Pan 128
Piaget, Jean 46
Pilgrim's Progress, The 52
Pinsent, Pat 48
Pleasants, Kathleen 145–146
political partisanship 87–88
politics 76–102
Postman, Neil 12
postcoloniality 71, 136, 138–142

posthumanism 146, 150–151
Potter, Beatrix 39, 83
Practical Education 58
propaganda 92–95
Pullman, Philip 2
Puritans 41, 42, 52, 87
'Purple Jar, The' 57–58, 59, 82

queerness 114, 122, 124–126

race 1, 3, 104, 114–119
racism 86, 91–92, 98–99, 114–117
Ratelle, Amy 149, 150
rational moralists 51, 57–58
reception memoirs 1, 5, 27, 28
Reese, Debbie 115
Reimer, Mavis 82–83
religion 47–48
Renaissance humanism 51
Resene, Michelle 127
Reynolds, Kimberley 14, 64, 72, 76, 77, 87, 120
Richardson, Alan 108
Rieder, John 74
Rioux, Anne Boyd 120–121
Robinson Crusoe 60
Robinson, Laura 124
Robinson, Peter 73
romanticism 57, 59–61, 65, 107, 146; and Hans Christian Andersen 70
Romines, Ann 101
Rose, Jacqueline 23, 25, 63, 139
Roth, Susan L. 137
Rouleau, Brian 29–30
Rousseau, Jean-Jacques 60, 106
Rowling, J. K. 30
Ruano, Alfonso 20
Rudd, David 23, 24, 50, 56, 58, 59
Rule, Stacy 147, 148
Russell, Bertrand 92
Ruys, Juanita Feros 50

Sánchez-Eppler, Karen 28–29, 43
Sands-O'Connor, Karen 68
Saunders, Kathy 127

schemas 109, 110
Schey, Ryan 125
Schwebel, Sara L. 29, 100
Sciurba, Katie 91
scripts 109, 110
Secret Diary of Adrian Mole, Aged 13¾, The 13
Sendak, Maurice 17, 26, 28, 82, 83, 140
Seuss, Dr. 96, 144–146
Sewell, Anna 62, 149
sexism 86
sexuality 3, 123, 125; and new materiality 126
Shakespeare, William 46
Sigler, Carolyn 142
Simon vs. the Homo Sapiens Agenda 125
Skármeta, Antonio 20
slavery 79–80
Smith Daniel, Jennifer 60–61
Smith-D'Arezzo, Wendy 104, 133, 135
Smith, Michelle 111
Snyder, Sharon L. 129, 154
social class 3
social hierarchies 80–82
socialization 76
Some Thoughts Concerning Education 54
Sommerville, C. John 87
Soviet Union 92, 93
Spufford, Francis 28
Spyri, Johanna 130
Steiner, Evgeny 93
Stephens, John 77, 83, 85
The Story of Ferdinand 90
Struwwelpeter (Shock-Headed Peter) 17
subversion 50, 76, 83–84, 156
Sumer, ancient 42–43

Tarr, Anita 123
Tatar, Maria 27
technological innovation 51, 64–65
Teorey, Matthew 145
Thein, Amanda Haertling 125
Thomas, Dylan 106, 107
Thomas, Ebony Elizabeth 115, 118
Thompson, Joyce 74

Thomson-Wohlgemuth, Gabrielle 93
Tintin au Congo (Hergé) 91
Token for Children, A 52–53
Tolkien, J. R. R. 28, 83
Tom Brown's Schooldays 44, 62, 124
Tommy Thumb's Pretty Song Book 54
Tougaw, Jason 112
Townsend, John Rowe 8
Townsend, Sue 13
Travers, P. L. 150
Trease, Geoffrey 87
Tribunella, Eric L. 123, 124, 154
trickster figures 20
Trites, Roberta Seelinger 26, 32–33, 109, 120, 123, 126, 152, 154
Trumbore, Cindy 137
Turner, Mark 109

Vaclavik, Kiera 71, 91
Vallone, Lynne 19
Verne, Jules 138
Vološinov, Valentin 24

Wall, Barbara 13
Wall, John 107–108
Wannamaker, Annette 121
Watership Down 10–11, 137, 148–149
Watts, Isaac 53, 62
'We Need Diverse Books' group 113
Westman, Karin E. 65–66
Wetta, Molly 34
What Katy Did 129
Where the Wild Things Are 17, 82, 140
White, E. B. 36–40
white supremacy 114–115
Wilder, Laura Ingalls 79, 97–102
Wild, Min 55
Williams, Abigail 12
Williams, Garth 39
Williams, James 73

Wimsatt, W. K. 12
The Wind in the Willows 148
Wollstonecraft, Mary 57
Wonder 130

Yang, Gene Luen 113, 120

young adult literature 30–33, 34; and new adult fiction 34

Xu, Xu 94

Zipes, Jack 21, 81–82

For Product Safety Concerns and Information please contact our EU representative GPSR@taylorandfrancis.com
Taylor & Francis Verlag GmbH, Kaufingerstraße 24, 80331 München, Germany

www.ingramcontent.com/pod-product-compliance
Lightning Source LLC
Chambersburg PA
CBHW071820230426
43670CB00013B/2513